THE HIGH-PROTEIN COOKBOOK

THE HIGH-PROTEIN COOKBOOK

by Linda West Eckhardt
and Katherine West DeFoyd

CLARKSON POTTER/PUBLISHERS
NEW YORK

Published by Clarkson Potter/Publishers, New York, New York.
Member of the Crown Publishing Group.

Random House, Inc. New York, Toronto, London, Sydney, Auckland
www.randomhouse.com

CLARKSON N. POTTER is a trademark and POTTER and colophon are registered trademarks of Random House, Inc.

Printed in the United States of America

Design by Maggie Hinders

Library of Congress Cataloging-in-Publication Data
Eckhardt, Linda West,
    The high-protein cookbook / by Linda West Eckhardt and Katherine West DeFoyd.
    Includes index.
    1. Cookery, American.   2. Low-carbohydrate diet—Recipes.   I. DeFoyd, Katherine West.
II. Title.
TX715.E178 2000
641.5′638—dc21

                                                                          00-037482

ISBN 0-609-80673-4

10   9   8   7   6   5   4   3   2

Dedication

To Bessie Lee Wood, mother and grandmother, who taught us the value of hard work, a nickel, and the importance of being thin.

Acknowledgments

This book was made possible by a few people who had the vision to see its value. First, thanks to Susan Ginsburg, our agent, who liked it well enough to *sell* it. Thank to Pam Krauss, our editor, who appreciates a fast and tasty low-carb dinner without "fake food," and who liked the book well enough to *buy* it.

Katherine would like to single out her father, who is a good role model for eating a balanced and healthy diet and staying thin. For her endeavors in both food and politics, his unconditional love and support were appreciated. She would also like to thank Gordon Murray, her husband, who is the best recipe tester and confidant a wife could have. Her two-year-old twins, Lily and Noel, provide us all with comic relief. And Prinolla Ramsunder, her au pair, always lends a helping hand and killer hot curry at just the right moment!

Linda would like to thank her husband, Joe. He is a great loving support and is always willing to try whatever she cooks. She would also like to thank all of the Eckhardt clan, who provide interesting family members and enough drama to keep life entertaining.

We'd both like to thank Cynthia LeGrone, food editor of *Country Living* magazine, for her unwavering support and strength.

Finally, thanks to all of our friends, who are understanding and still our friends, even when we can't begin to call them back or make plans for months on end because of book deadlines, book tours, corporate spokesperson work, and all of the other distractions of life in the new millennium.

Contents

THE HIGH-PROTEIN COOKBOOK

Introduction

So you've been on a high-protein diet. Or know people who rave about the good results they've gotten by limiting their carbohydrates. But you're not sure if you can live on nothing but steaks and nibbles of lettuce.

Well, we had the same concerns. We're a mother-daughter cookbook writing team who—for a variety of reasons—had gained more weight than we were comfortable with.

Our love of great food and our various age issues made weight gain seem inevitable. Being food scholars, we read everything we could about the new wave of dieting plans. We also read all the criticism that comes from the legitimate food press.

The good news is that by following a high-protein diet, we each lost more than twenty-five pounds. The bad news is that we got really bored with the scant recipes offered in the sources we consulted. Because food boredom is all too often the undoing of what begins as a successful diet regimen, we began to put our professional expertise to work on this very personal problem. We developed a group of recipes that made this diet acceptable to us. We are living proof that you can eat well—really well—lose weight, improve your health, and feel great.

The High-Protein Cookbook is not a diet book. No diet works for everyone, and you should certainly consult with your physician before making any significant change in the way you eat. *The High-Protein Cookbook* was conceived as a companion to today's popular high-protein diet books. Whether you follow Eades, the Zone, Sugar Busters, or others in this genre, you'll find recipes in this cookbook that offer you fast and fresh ideas to keep you on your diet and help you in your quest to lose weight and get healthy. At the same time, you'll be preparing varied, interesting meals that everyone in the household will enjoy, so there's no need to serve one meal for yourself and another for family members who don't feel the need to limit their carbohydrates.

These recipes adhere to strict nutritional guidelines—that is, no more than 15 grams of carbohydrate per meal, and a daily caloric intake that hovers around 1,500. You'll also find recipes that encourage you to eat those healthy vegetables and fruits, at least five a day. And mostly, you'll find *reasonable* amounts of high-quality protein—3 to 4 ounces of lean, cooked red meats, and up to 6 ounces of fish per meal. Complete nutritional analyses for each recipe was calculated using ESHA Research Inc., National Restaurant Association's computer program, allow you to budget carbohydrates and calories.

But the most important distinction we make is that our recipes taste good. With us, taste *is* number one. If our dinners don't have exciting flavor profiles, we know we'll never stick with any change in eating patterns. This book is a short course in high-protein cooking. The recipes use a short list of fast and fresh ingredients with clear instructions. The recipes are simple enough for the beginner cook and interesting enough for experts. Best of all, you don't have to rely on fake foods or phony processed diet dinners to get your weight under control. You can use real food, real cooking techniques, and you can have dinner on the table in a hurry—in 30 minutes or less.

WHY HIGH PROTEIN?

After fifteen years of carbo loading, a period in which Americans have watched one another getting fatter and fatter, we've decided to face facts: Empty calories will eventually equal extra pounds. Like numerous others, we found that by eliminating many of the carbohydrate-rich foods that formed the backbone of our diets and boosting our intake of lean protein, we not only lost weight, we felt better, had more energy, and saw some pretty significant changes in our blood cholesterol levels. Across the country people are embracing a diet based less on overly refined carbohydrates and more on lean protein, fruits, and vegetables, and they are seeing positive results. It has benefited so many, in fact, that we believe a fundamental shift away from excess carbohydrates will prevail, just as our understanding of the role of saturated fats has caused a sea change in the way America eats.

We want to make one thing clear. It doesn't take a doctor to tell you that a diet consisting entirely of enormous grilled steaks or chicken breasts with green salads on the side will not sustain good health. In fact, it can lead to serious health risks. That's why we've pursued a moderate path. Our recipes preclude the dangers of a radical protein diet, which potentially puts the body into a state of ketosis, by incorporating generous amounts of healthy vegetables and fruits. You'll see that all of our recipes include a protein *and* vegetable or, at the very least, a vegetable suggestion. We truly believe the best shot at good nutrition is to eat a wide and varied diet of unprocessed foods, including sufficient protein for health and endurance, and five vegetables and fruits every day to provide the best quality of *complex* carbohydrates, vitamins, minerals, and sufficient fiber for optimum health.

A Word About Portion Size

In order to lose weight, we do have to count calories. They are nothing more than the energy units necessary to fuel our own personal furnaces. When we feed our machines excess energy, our bodies use what they need and store the rest for a rainy day in the form of fat.

The recipes in this book do not offer unhealthy, outsized portions. Three to 4 ounces of meat or up to 6 ounces of fish provide more than enough protein and are sufficient to keep you satisfied until your next meal. In restaurants today, it is not uncommon for each diner to be presented with 8, 10, or even

12 ounces of protein, and a meal that represents about 2,500 calories overall. This is absurd. Unless you are able to radically increase your daily exercise output, you will not lose weight if your caloric intake exceeds about 1,500 *per day.*

All of our recipes indicate clearly what a portion size should look like. Should you find yourself staring at a typically gargantuan restaurant serving, here's an easy no-scale way to judge how much you should eat: Look at the palm of your hand. A 3- to 4-ounce portion of meat or fish is about that size. If there's more than that much protein on your plate, cut some off and hand it to your dining companion, or put it in a "doggie bag" for a free lunch the next day. If you follow a high-protein diet, you can do this without feeling hungry because the body takes longer to digest protein. Protein "sticks to your ribs."

Add one cup of leafy green vegetables, ¾ cup cooked vegetables, plus medium-size pieces of fruit (oranges, apples, and pears), or 1 cup of berries. Fruits and vegetables give you needed fiber, which protects the bowel. It's like your mama said: Eat your vegetables.

The body is a wonderfully adaptable machine. Just as it has adjusted to your former bad eating habits, given half a chance, the body will adapt and quit crying out for cookies and cakes. Then you are more than halfway to success. Eat sufficient protein, balance it off with a generous serving of the right vegetables and fruits, and you will succeed.

When There's No Time to Cook

Don't even have time to look at a recipe? You belong to a huge club; some would say an enormous society. In fact, if you think we use recipes every night to make terrific meals, you have a fantasy about the life of a food writer. Many a night, we do nothing but grill or sauté a chop, rip open a bag of salad, and eat. Part of this new way of life is making food less central to your existence.

We can teach you how to improve your skills with a sauté pan and grill so that you'll soon be whipping up sweet little suppers without cracking a book. That's what we're here for.

Yes, you may have to break the muffin–breakfast cereal–sugary doughnut habit. Those convenience foods have come to dominate America's breakfast and the cessation of that habit may be the most important change you make. Stop the hypoglycemic yo-yo that starts with a big jolt of sugar for breakfast, and you've made a heroic beginning on a high-protein plan.

Eating the Rest of the Day

The recipes in *The High-Protein Cookbook* are intended primarily as dinner entrees, although many could be made in larger quantities and served for lunch the next day. We recommend that you decide on a basic breakfast and lunch strategy and simply stick with it, day in, day out, saving your energy, creativity, and best recipes for the evening meal. Before you protest that this will be too limiting, think about what you eat for breakfast now—it's probably just as limited a menu. Do *not* skip breakfast; simply substitute a healthy, high-protein option, such as cottage cheese and berries, or eggs with a piece of thin toast, or even a cheese omelet. Make that your "regular" and be done with it. Soon it will feel as natural as that bagel "with a smear" or that bowl of oatmeal does now. Make sure you get sufficient protein at every meal. Eat five vegetables and fruits every day and drink lots and lots of water—at *least* 64 ounces per day. Load your refrigerator and purse with acceptable emergency provisions, such as string cheese, hard-cooked eggs, and hard salami. If you're so hungry you can't wait for dinner, spread a tablespoon of chunky natural peanut butter on a couple of celery ribs and munch away. It's about 6 grams of carbohydrates and quite satisfying. And don't forget, a glass of red wine has been shown to promote good cardiac health. So eat well, drink wisely, and feel good about realigning your eating habits into a more healthful, life-affirming pattern.

THE QUESTION OF VITAMINS

Supplements have gained acceptance among professional nutritionists, medical doctors, and dieticians. The old argument that you should get all the vitamins you need from your diet seems to have melted away. We believe a sound supplementation program, in addition to your new dietary regimen, can only increase your health benefits and make you stronger and more vigorous. For openers, we recommend a good all-purpose multivitamin. Don't snatch up the cheapest bottle you see on sale. Read the label. Pick a multivitamin that includes both vitamins and minerals and reasonable amounts of the additives that promote health.

The National Academy of Science Food and Nutrition Board calls thirteen vitamins and ten minerals "essential." This government body sets recommended dietary allowances (RDAs) for men and women of various ages. In theory, if you are eating the recommended number of servings from the five food groups, including at least five servings of fruits and vegetables, you should be getting all the vitamins and minerals you need.

But you know the difference between theory and practice. A 1994 USDA survey found most adult women failed to meet the RDAs for iron, zinc, vitamin B6, calcium, magnesium, and vitamin E, while men were short on zinc and magnesium. While this diet goes far to ameliorate these deficiencies, with its emphasis on red meat, eggs, fish, and a variety of green leafy vegetables, we recommend a daily multivitamin/mineral supplement. Think of it as an insurance policy.

You must understand that RDAs were established a number of years ago, and were intended only to prevent nutrient shortages that lead to ailments such as scurvy or rickets. Antioxidants—which scientists now believe act as scavengers for oxygen-free radicals responsible for harmful cellular changes leading to cancer, heart disease, and other disorders—are best supplemented.

Vitamin E can boost the immune system and promote heart health, among many other things. Tufts University's vitamin E researcher, Jeffrey Blumberg, Ph.D., a professor of nutrition, recommends a daily intake of 100 to 400 IUs (international units) of supplemental vitamin E for healthy people, and 400 to 800 IUs for those who have heart disease or diabetes. We faithfully take our 400-IU dose of Vitamin E.

Vitamin C has a recommended RDA of 60 milligrams. But scientists believe between 250 and 500 milligrams are beneficial for general health. Up to 1,000 milligrams may be taken before stomach upsets or other counterproductive effects are felt. We like a couple of 500-milligram chewables a day.

Beta-carotene is a plant-based antioxidant your body can transform into vitamin A as needed. You can take up to 5,000 IUs with no unpleasant side effects.

Folic acid and vitamins B12 and B6 are linked to a lower incidence of heart disease and heart attacks. You need at least 400 micrograms. You'll get a lot from meat and eggs, but supplementation is recommended, particularly if you are of child-bearing age.

Calcium builds strong bones and teeth and reduces our risk for osteoporosis. The high-protein diet contains lots of calcium if you eat eggs and cheese, but the Nutrition Board has raised the RDA for adults up to the age of fifty to 1,000 milligrams, and to 1,200 milligrams for those over fifty. The average woman gets only about 600 milligrams of calcium in her normal diet, so a supplement of 1,000 milligrams is advised.

Vitamin D, the sunshine vitamin, available in milk, butter, and egg yolks, potentiates the use of calcium. The recommended RDA is 200 IUs, but 400 IUs are recommended as supplementation for adults between the ages of fifty and seventy because after fifty, the body may not absorb dietary sources as well.

In addition to the vitamins and minerals listed above, trace minerals, including magnesium, iron, and selenium, are needed by the body but are usually found in adequate supply in a good all-purpose multivitamin.

To Learn More

If you'd like to calculate your own recipes, do what we did. Order the National Restaurant Association Nutrition Recipe Analysis, Version 1.0, from ESHA Research. This well-respected computer program will tell you what you need to know. Call ESHA (503-585-5543) or e-mail them (nra@esha.com).

Two 5-feet-4-inch women, each of whom weigh 140 pounds, may look quite different. One seems fat and the other just right. Why? Body mass index. How much fat do you carry? How much in muscle and bone? Learn your own BMI (body mass index), and you'll get a scientific recommendation of the correct weight for your height and body frame size. The simplest way to determine this is to go online and let one of the computer analysts do the work for you. Try *www.thriveonline.com/shape/experts/karen/karen.* However, if you are good at math, you can figure this out for yourself. Here's how to calculate your own BMI: Multiply your weight in pounds by 704.5, and then divide by the square of your height in inches. For example, if you weigh 130 pounds and are 5 feet 4 inches (64 inches) tall, then your BMI is (130 × 704.5) ÷ (64 × 64) = 22.4.

So what, you say? If your BMI is 27 or below, your health is not at risk from fat, but if it's above that number, you have jumped into the high-risk category for coronary heart disease, stroke, and certain cancers.

Three sisters, who have dieted successfully, started a Web site that acts as a clearinghouse for lots of great information: nutrition analysis, BMI and basal metabolism calculations, and lots more. Log onto *3fatchicks.com*. You'll find lots of good answers by going through this gateway.

You can also call the American Dietetic Association (800-366-1655) and ask for their free brochures. To order a free copy of the USDA brochure "Nutrition and Your Health: Dietary Guidelines for Americans," call the Centrum Center for Nutritional Science (800-597-2267).

EQUIPMENT AND SUPPLIES

High-protein cooking does not require any unusual appliances or expensive equipment. In fact, you are likely to have all that you need already. Here are the items we find indispensable.

Sauté pan: A good-quality nonstick 10- to 12-inch skillet will get you through most of the meals in this book.

Steamer: Linda constantly uses her steamer for vegetable accompaniments.

Grilling machine: A secret weapon in the armament of high-protein cooks. We each keep one on the counter. In almost any recipe, foods that are to be sautéed can also be grilled, and this is one quick and easy way to do it. Others we know swear by their **stove-top water-pan grill**, which uses your stove's burners as its heat source. The water below the grill surface reduces the smoky fumes released into your kitchen.

Citrus zester: Want to zip up flavor? Add zest from almost any citrus fruit—lemon, lime, or orange—to whatever you're cooking, and you'll get a flavor hit that's memorable. To make it even easier, invest in a **Microplane,** the newest and best piece of equipment to come along for zipping up flavor. You can also use it to grate ginger or garlic, or to add a dusting of nutmeg. Look for it at the cookware store. For about twelve bucks, you'll get a new magic wand.

Kitchen scale (or diet scale): Keeps you honest with food portions. You'll note that when possible, we give measurements in ounces for carbohydrate-rich foods that might sabotage your efforts. Most scales come with their own food tray and measure in both grams and ounces. A scale takes the guesswork out of measurement.

Sports bottle: You must drink at least 64 ounces of water a day to help flush all the fat and toxins away. Fill your bottle each morning and carry it with you throughout the day. It's especially recommended if you sit at a desk all day. Choose your water. We like seltzer. You may like spring water. Just pick a clean, pure water to drink.

FISH: YOUR NEW BEST FRIEND

Fish belongs

on everyone's menu, not just those on a low-carbohydrate diet. It is naturally low in fat, flavorful, and full of essential vitamins (including many vitamin Bs), minerals (especially iodine and phosphorus), and in particular, omega-3 fatty acids, which lower triglycerides, act as anticoagulants, and lower insulin levels. In plain English, fish is good for you. We also love fish for the same reason restaurateurs do: it cooks fast. The fact is, if you are on a high-protein regimen, fish gives great bang for the buck. It may cost more than chicken or pork pound for pound, but because it is not as dense as red meat or fowl, a 6-ounce fillet is larger than a 6-ounce piece of steak. You *feel* like you are eating more. It may only be a psychological advantage, but hey, we will take any advantage we can get.

Which leads us to the main point about fish. It is a great weapon with which to fight our biggest dieting battle, food boredom. In the first place, more than sixty varieties of fish enter the marketplace in this country on any given day. When you multiply the number of varieties of fish times the number of ways you can cook and season it, you could probably eat fish every day for the rest of your life and never get bored.

With all of its great qualities, you may be wondering why is it that we most often order fish in a restaurant and not at the fish market. We figure it is fear of getting bad fish, plus not enough information on how to prepare this delicate protein source.

When cooking fish, know that it's more important to purchase the freshest variety you can get, rather than the exact species called for in the recipe. Only purchase fish from vendors who keep their wares on ice, and who make at least twice-weekly trips to their wholesale source. (In our experience, Tuesdays and Fridays are when markets get their supplies.) Lastly, always cook fish the day you get it—it's that fragile.

If you're buying a whole fish, ask the fishmonger to clean it for you. Choose a fish with bright, clear eyes. Sunken, cloudy eyes means it's past its prime. Never hesitate to ask for a sniff. Any odor of ammonia means the fish is gone. If you're buying fillets, ask the fishmonger when he got them in; if they've been frozen (not necessarily a bad thing); and ask for a sniff. If the layers of meat are gaping, the fish is over the hill. The meat should look firm, shiny, and clear. It should also smell briny and fresh—not fishy or of ammonia. Ask the fishmonger to double wrap the fish, putting ice in the outside plastic bag. Keep it on ice, double bagged in the refrigerator, until you're ready to cook later that day.

Contrary to what some people think, the best time of year to eat shellfish is in the winter. Any fisherman will tell you that as the oceans get colder, the fish tastes better. Most Gulf Coast natives (us included) will only eat shellfish in the months with an "r" in it. And we are suspicious of September. Nearly all shrimp is frozen the minute it is caught. So if you can buy it frozen in 5-pound blocks, you have more control over when it is defrosted. This is how restaurateurs and caterers buy it. Just remember to give the shrimp enough time to thaw—overnight in the refrigerator or in cold water. Partial defrosting to break off what you need is okay, too, and preferable to buying thawed shrimp.

The other problem most home cooks have with fish is that they tend to overcook it. Fish and shellfish cook very quickly. When overcooked, they become dry and rubbery. They are not chicken. They do not need to be well-done. As you begin to buy and cook fish and shellfish more often, you will increase your comfort level. Make a regular date to stop by the fish counter, preferably the day the major shipment comes in (not Sunday night). Soon, cooking fish will be become very easy.

Lastly, remember a recipe is only a guide. If the recipe calls for cod and the store only has mahimahi, then feel free to substitute. Perhaps it is seafood's versatility that makes it the most valuable. Go forth and eat fish.

Sea Bass with Mango Chutney, Ginger, and Black Sesame Seeds

The buttery flavor of sea bass is a delicious complement to the chutney, ginger, and sesame. Serve over a crunchy bed of shredded iceberg lettuce.

MAKES 2 SERVINGS

Preparation time: 5 minutes

Baking time: 15 minutes

Cooking spray

Two 6-ounce sea bass fillets

1 tablespoon minced fresh ginger (see note)

1 tablespoon soy sauce

1 teaspoon sesame oil

Salt and freshly milled black pepper to taste

¼ cup mango chutney

3 cups shredded iceberg lettuce

Ginger and Hot Red Pepper Vinaigrette
(page 131)

Preheat the oven to 425°F. Spray an 8 × 8 × 8-inch Pyrex baking dish with cooking spray. Place the fillets in the baking dish. Sprinkle each fillet with ginger, soy sauce, and sesame oil. Lightly salt and pepper. Cover the dish with foil and bake for 10 minutes. Remove from the oven and spoon 2 tablespoons of chutney onto each fillet. Return to the oven and bake, uncovered, for 5 more minutes.

Toss the shredded lettuce with the dressing. Divide between two plates and top each one with a fillet.

Nutritional Analysis: 316 calories, FAT 10 g, PROTEIN 40 g, CARB 15 g, FIBER 6 g, CHOL 90 mg, IRON 1 mg, SODIUM 1,258 mg, CALC 32 mg

Cooking Lesson

Fresh ginger can easily be minced in a food processor. Don't bother peeling, Asians never do! Place 1-inch chunks in the food processor and process until coarsely chopped; do not overchop. To store, place in a jar with a tight-fitting lid and pour in dry sherry until the ginger is just covered. Ginger will keep for at least 6 months in your refrigerator this way, and it's ready when you are!

Roasted Striped Bass on a Bed of Summer Vegetables

Caramelized vegetables make a flavorful bed for one of the Northeast's favorite fish. Can't find striped bass? Choose a firm-fleshed white fish, such as cod, haddock, or halibut.

MAKES 2 SERVINGS

Preparation time: 5 minutes
Cooking time: 30–35 minutes

2 tablespoons extra-virgin olive oil

1 yellow crookneck squash, sliced into thin coins

1 small zucchini, sliced into thin coins

½ fennel bulb, thinly sliced

1 small red onion, peeled and quartered

1 tablespoon tarragon vinegar

3 garlic cloves, peeled and smashed

½ teaspoon dried thyme

¼ teaspoon kosher salt, plus additional for sprinkling

Two 6-ounce striped bass fillets, or other firm-fleshed white fish, such as haddock, halibut, or cod

Freshly milled black pepper

½ cup fresh basil leaves, cut in ribbons

Preheat the oven to 450° F. Film a large ovenproof skillet with 2 teaspoons of the olive oil, then add the yellow squash, zucchini, fennel, and onion. Toss with a tablespoon of the olive oil, vinegar, garlic, thyme, and salt. Roast for 20 minutes.

While the vegetables are cooking, brush the fish fillets with the remaining teaspoon of olive oil and season with salt and pepper. Stir the vegetables. Lay the fish on top and cook until the fish flakes easily, 5 to 10 minutes more. To serve, make a bed of vegetables on two warm plates and top with a fish fillet. Mound half the basil ribbons on each fillet.

Nutritional Analysis: 400 calories, FAT 19 g, PROTEIN 42 g, CARB 14 g, FIBER 5 g, CHOL 175 mg, IRON 3 mg, SODIUM 476 mg, CALC 117 mg

Health Benefit

Summer squashes, such as zucchini, crooknecks, and pattypans, are considered "free" vegetables. Eat all you want for optimum fiber and vitamins, as well as great taste.

Braised Monkfish with Fennel and Pernod

This recipe torques up the anise flavor with fennel, fennel seed, and Pernod. The result is surprisingly subtle, and very French.

MAKES 2 SERVINGS

Preparation time: 10 minutes

Cooking time: 20 minutes

¼ cup olive oil

½ cup chopped onion

¼ pound sliced fennel bulb

1 teaspoon fennel seeds

1 garlic clove, minced

1 cup dry white wine

One 8-ounce bottle clam juice

One 8-ounce can tomatoes with their juices, chopped

1 tablespoon Pernod

12 ounces monkfish fillets, skinned

1 tablespoon finely chopped fresh curly-leaf parsley for garnish

In a large skillet with a tight-fitting lid, heat the oil over medium-high heat. Add the onion, fennel, fennel seeds, and garlic and sauté until the onions are translucent, about 10 minutes. Add the white wine and clam juice and deglaze the pan, scraping up brown bits from the bottom. Boil until the wine and juice are reduced by half, about 5 minutes. Stir in the tomatoes with their juices and Pernod and add the monkfish fillets. Cover and simmer for 5 minutes. Serve fish, vegetables, and broth in soup plates sprinkled with freshly chopped parsley.

Nutritional Analysis: 242 calories, FAT 3 g, PROTEIN 27 g, CARB 14 g, FIBER 4 g, CHOL 43 mg, IRON 2 mg, SODIUM 207 mg, CALC 93 mg

Cooking Lesson

MONKFISH: Known in France and in French restaurants as *lotte,* this is a delicious, firm-fleshed fish that tastes a bit like shellfish. It is sometimes called "poor man's lobster," but in our opinion, you are rich with this delicacy on your table!

PERNOD (PER NOH): A yellowish, milky liqueur with a licorice flavor. In the old days, people used absinthe, from the wormwood family, but since it's actually a poison, it fell into disfavor. Often Pernod is the secret ingredient in bouillabaisse, oysters Rockefeller, and other New Orleans dishes.

Steamed Cod in Borscht with Warm Chive-Horseradish Cream

There are few better ways to infuse fish fillets with flavor than by steaming them atop aromatic vegetables. The aroma that wafts up from a steaming bowl of fish swimming in a sea of cabbage and beets will more than make up for the fact that this looks like an estuary after the powerboats have chewed through the water lilies. Never mind. Go ahead. Taste it.

Preparation time: 7 minutes
Cooking time: 13 minutes

MAKES 2 SERVINGS

1 teaspoon peanut oil

½ cup thinly sliced red onion

1 garlic clove, sliced

½ teaspoon dried thyme

2 tablespoons minced fresh flat-leaf parsley

½ cup shredded savoy cabbage

¼ cup drained and julienned canned beets

2 cups low-sodium chicken broth

Two 6-ounce cod steaks or fillets (or other firm-fleshed white fish, such as Chilean sea bass, haddock, halibut)

¼ teaspoon kosher salt, or to taste

½ teaspoon freshly milled black pepper, or to taste

1 tablespoon minced fresh chives

1 tablespoon prepared horseradish

2 tablespoons sour cream

Heat a heavy pot, then film the bottom with oil. Add the onion and garlic and sauté over medium-high heat until the onion becomes translucent, about 3 minutes. Stir in the thyme, parsley, cabbage, beets, and chicken broth and bring to a boil over medium heat. Cover and simmer for 5 minutes. Uncover the pot and arrange the cod on top of the vegetables; season to taste with salt and pepper. Cover and steam the fish until cooked through, about 5 minutes. Meanwhile, stir together the chives, horseradish, and sour cream in a small bowl.

To serve, ladle some of the vegetables and broth into a warm wide-rimmed soup bowl and top with a steamed fish steak. Add a dollop of chive-horseradish cream.

Nutritional Analysis: 255 calories, FAT 9 g, PROTEIN 34 g, CARB 10 g, FIBER 2 g, CHOL 69 mg, IRON 1 mg, SODIUM 1,198 mg, CALC 62 mg

Cooking Lesson

By steaming fish on top of the simmering vegetables and broth, you'll get the benefit of the aromatic steam and enhance the broth as well, losing not one precious drop of flavor.

Health Benefit

The monounsaturated fatty acids in mayonnaise and olive oil help prevent heart disease. This dinner makes the most of their health-promoting properties. Olive oil, which is one of the top-choice fats, starts the process by caramelizing the vegetables to concentrate their naturally occurring sugars. Then the oil in the cold-water fish, cod, tops it off, giving you a meal that tastes great and is loaded with natural antioxidants: cabbage, onions, and beets. Toss in the fiber you get from the vegetables and you have here an almost perfect dinner.

Roasted Cod with Clementine Sauce on a Bed of Braised Brussels Sprouts

Citrus is one of winter's gifts. For a delicate sauce that flatters a cod, use the juice of Spain's clementine. (Substitute a tangerine or Florida orange in a pinch.) The main satisfaction to this dish is that you get every flavor note at once: sweet, sour, bitter, and salty. First the sweetness of the fruit, then the pucker from the undercurrent of acid, a warming trend of cayenne, and the bracing bitter flavor found in the Brussels sprouts—all of this in addition to the sweet-salty codfish.

Preparation time: 15 minutes
Cooking time: 15 minutes

MAKES 2 SERVINGS

1 tablespoon olive oil
2 cups finely sliced Brussels sprouts (about 1 pint)
Grated zest and juice of 1 clementine
12 ounces cod fillets or other firm, mild, cold-water white fish
Pinch of cayenne
½ teaspoon kosher salt
1 tablespoon unsalted butter
1 tablespoon minced fresh cilantro

Preheat the oven to 500°F. Heat a saucepan over medium-high heat and film the bottom with some of the oil. Sauté Brussels sprouts about 3 minutes. Reserve 2 tablespoons of the clementine juice, and pour the rest into a small saucepan. Boil over medium-high heat until reduced by half (about 5 minutes). Add the reserved juice to the Brussels sprouts, cover, and steam about 3 minutes. Keep warm.

Place a large ovenproof skillet or gratin dish on the stovetop and preheat over high heat. Film it with the remaining olive oil, then add the fish. Cook 1 minute, then carefully turn the fish. Transfer to the oven and cook until the fish flakes, no more than 5 to 8 minutes.

Season the reduced citrus juice with zest, cayenne, and salt. Off heat, swirl in the butter, whisking until the sauce is thick.

To serve, divide Brussels sprouts between two warmed dinner plates, then top each with a fish fillet. Spoon the sauce over and garnish with the cilantro.

Nutritional Analysis: 278 calories, FAT 9 g, PROTEIN 34 g, CARB 15 g, FIBER 4 g, CHOL 78 mg, IRON 2 mg, SODIUM 776 mg, CALC 64 mg

Cooking Lesson

Zip up meals using citrus zest, a nearly calorie-free flavor enhancer. Buy one of those new Microplane rasps, and it's all too easy. One pass of the fruit skin over the rasp and you have a neat, flavorful bite, plus the colorful oil of citrus, which lifts up many a plain food. Regardless of the tool you use to zest, take care not to bear down into the pithy white underflesh, which is bitter. All you want is color and flavor.

Menu Suggestion

Once in awhile, nothing but chocolate will do. For a ravishing 5-gram carb finish to this meal, take your choice: Melt a Hershey's Nugget on your tongue. Want crunch? Chew on eight Starbucks chocolate-covered espresso beans. Need a kiss? Take two Hershey's kisses with almonds. With this menu, you can afford it.

Grilled Halibut with Anchovy-Lemon Butter

People may think they don't like anchovies, but when used as a flavor enhancer, as in this savory butter, it's a simple addition that adds a subtle taste. Always use the canned variety rather than the salted, or use the paste. If your market doesn't have halibut you can freely interchange with other cold-water ocean fishes—salmon, swordfish.

MAKES 2 SERVINGS

Preparation time: 5 minutes
Cooking time: 10 to 12 minutes

½ teaspoon extra-virgin olive oil

Two 6-ounce halibut steaks

½ teaspoon kosher salt

½ teaspoon cracked pepper

2 teaspoons softened unsalted butter

1 tablespoon anchovy paste or 1 tablespoon chopped canned anchovy

Zest of 1 lemon plus 1 tablespoon fresh lemon juice

Preheat a large skillet, then film it with oil. Meanwhile, pat the fish steaks dry, then salt and pepper them. Brush each side with a little oil then place in the skillet and cook about 4 minutes per side.

Meanwhile, stir together the butter, anchovy paste, zest, and lemon juice in a small bowl. Transfer the steaks to warmed dinner plates and top with a dollop of anchovy butter.

Nutritional Analysis: 236 calories, FAT 9 g, PROTEIN 36 g, CARB. 2 g, FIBER .5 g, CHOL 65 mg, IRON 2 mg, SODIUM 745 mg, CALC 90 mg

Health Benefit

Choose cold-water ocean fish several times a week You'll increase your intake of EPA, an omega-3 fatty acid found in fish oils that helps prevent heart disease. Which are the cold-water ocean fishes? Cod, salmon, mackerel, herring, halibut, and other less well-known fishes. If you can't include fish often enough, take cod liver oil pills by mouth, but be aware that it takes three or four a day to equal one good fish dinner.

The Halibut Caper

Pan-frying fish is about the quickest, easiest way we know to get food on the table. Finish the crisp, golden fillet with a lemon-caper sauce, and you can call it a party. Dredge fillets in salt, pepper, and flour. Shake off any excess. Pan-fry in oil you've splashed into the skillet, then finish with a jot of chicken broth, a shot of lemon juice, a spoonful of capers and a pat of butter. Voilá. A French classic.

Preparation time: 10 minutes
Cooking time: 5 minutes

MAKES 2 SERVINGS

½ teaspoon salt

½ teaspoon freshly milled black pepper

1 tablespoon all-purpose flour

½ cup low-sodium chicken broth

Grated zest and juice of 1 lemon

1 tablespoon drained capers

1 tablespoon peanut oil

Two 6-ounce boneless, skinless halibut fillets

1 tablespoon butter

Stir together the salt, pepper, and flour on a piece of wax paper. Mix the broth, lemon, and capers in a small cup. Heat a large skillet over medium-high heat, then film the bottom with oil. Dredge the fish in the seasoned flour, then cook until it is light brown on the bottom, about 2 minutes. Flip it over, adding oil if necessary to keep it from sticking, and cook the second side until browned, about 2 minutes. Transfer to warmed dinner plates. Crank up the heat under the skillet and pour in the lemon-caper mixture. Scrape up the brown bits in the skillet and boil it down until somewhat reduced. Remove from the heat, and swirl in the butter. Pour the sauce over the fish and serve.

Nutritional Analysis: 443 calories, FAT 29 g, PROTEIN 38 g, CARB 7 g, FIBER 2 g, CHOL 90 mg, IRON 2 mg, SODIUM 1,183 mg, CALC 175 mg

Mahimahi on a Bed of Roasted Red Peppers

The firm texture and subtle flavor of mahimahi juxtaposed with the smooth texture and sweet flavor of roasted red pepper is a winner every time. For a beautiful meal, serve along with roasted yellow squash.

Preparation time: 5 minutes
Cooking time: 15 minutes

MAKES 2 SERVINGS

1 cup roasted red bell pepper, chopped **(see note)**

1 clove garlic, minced

¼ teaspoon cumin

1 tablespoon fresh lemon juice

1½ teaspoons extra-virgin olive oil

12 ounces mahimahi fillets

½ teaspoon salt

½ teaspoon freshly milled black pepper

Preheat the oven to 425°F. Spray an 8 × 8-inch Pyrex baking dish with cooking spray or oil lightly. Stir the red pepper, garlic, cumin, lemon juice, and 1 teaspoon of the olive oil into the dish. Lay mahimahi fillets on top and brush with the remaining oil. Season lightly with salt and pepper. Cover tightly with aluminum foil. Bake for 12 to 15 minutes, just until the fish is opaque. Scoop red pepper and fish onto warmed dinner plate. Nestle a mound of roasted yellow squash alongside.

Nutritional Analysis, including the Squash: 205 calories, FAT 5 g, PROTEIN 32 g, CARB 4 g, FIBER .3 g, CHOL 124 mg, IRON 4 mg, SODIUM 854 mg, CALC 36 mg

Cooking Lesson

If you don't have time to roast your own peppers, try to buy them from the fresh deli section of a quality grocery stores; they are better than the peppers in a jar. If you want to make your own, roast peppers directly over a gas flame or in a 450°F. oven, turning, until skin is charred all over. Pop into a paper bag, seal, and let the peppers sweat a few minutes. Strip skin off and discard. Remove and discard seed and pulp. Cut roasted pepper flesh into strips. This will add about 15 minutes to your overall cooking time.

Roasted Yellow Squash with Lemon Juice

MAKES 2 SERVINGS

Preparation time: 5 minutes
Cooking time: 15 minutes

4 yellow summer squash, sliced ¼ inch thick

2 tablespoons extra-virgin olive oil

1 tablespoon fresh lemon juice

Salt and freshly milled black pepper to taste

Preheat the oven to 425° F. Toss the squash with the olive oil, lemon juice, and salt and pepper. Spread out in a single layer in a large 9 × 13 × 2-inch glass baking pan. Bake until golden brown, about 15 minutes. Serve warm or cold.

Chilled Hawaiian Mahimahi with Lomi-Lomi Relish

Make this dish at your convenience and refrigerate, then serve cold or at room temperature. It's especially good in the summer when you don't even want to think about heating up the kitchen.

MAKES 2 SERVINGS

Preparation time: 15 minutes

Cooking time: 10 minutes

Chilling time: 30 minutes to 24 hours

LOMI-LOMI RELISH

¼ cup finely chopped cherry tomatoes

¼ cup finely chopped yellow bell pepper

1 scallion, finely sliced

2 tablespoons minced onion

1 tablespoon minced jalapeño

1 tablespoon fresh lemon juice

½ teaspoon salt

12 ounces mahimahi fillets

2 bay leaves

½ teaspoon black peppercorns

Grated zest of ½ lemon plus 1 tablespoon fresh lemon juice

Romaine lettuce leaves

Stir together the relish ingredients in a small bowl: tomatoes, bell pepper, scallion, yellow onion, jalapeño, lemon juice, and salt. Cover and refrigerate until serving time.

Place a steamer rack inside a large pan of simmering water. Line the rack with wet cheesecloth or parchment paper. Place the fish on the cloth and top with the bay leaves and peppercorns. Squeeze lemon juice over all and sprinkle with grated lemon zest. Cover and steam about 10 minutes, or just until the fish flakes. Use the cheesecloth or paper to transfer the fish to a large plate. Cover and refrigerate until serving time.

To serve, arrange romaine lettuce leaves on a chilled dinner plate, add the fish, and top with some of the relish.

Nutritional Analysis: 173 calories, FAT 2 g, PROTEIN 33 g, CARB 7 g, FIBER 2 g, CHOL 124 mg, IRON 3 mg, SODIUM 738 mg, CALC 50 mg

Cooking Lesson

Steaming is an excellent method for cooking sushi-quality fish. In other words, be extra careful that the fish you cook is pristinely fresh. The delicate flavor of the fish will shine through.

Menu Suggestion

Add a ¾-cup serving of strawberries with whipped cream for dessert, and you will have added no more than 5 grams of carbs to create a totally satisfying meal.

Roasted Oysters with Spinach, Pernod, and Orange Mayonnaise

You'll like this sophisticated first dish best if you begin with fresh baby spinach—the kind in the cellophane package that doesn't even require washing. But you can also use regular fresh or frozen spinach. You'll need to wash the regular kind in a big bowl of ice water to remove the sand; if you use frozen, you'll just have to thaw it. But trust us. Baby spinach is the best.

Preparation time: 10 minutes
Cooking time: 15 minutes

MAKES 2 SERVINGS

1 tablespoon extra-virgin olive oil
Grated zest from ½ orange plus ¼ cup fresh
    orange juice
½ cup mayonnaise

12 ounces baby spinach
1 teaspoon minced garlic
2 teaspoons Pernod
12 fresh oysters

Preheat the oven to 500° F. Coat two small gratin dishes or one medium baking dish with some of the olive oil and set them aside. Stir orange juice and zest into mayonnaise.

Preheat a large skillet over medium-high heat. Film the bottom with the remaining olive oil. Add the spinach and sauté, stirring, until spinach is just wilted, about 1 minute. Remove from the heat and stir in the garlic and Pernod.

Divide the spinach between the ramekins or arrange it in a baking dish. Top with the oysters. Add a dab of orange mayonnaise to the top of each oyster and bake just until the mayonnaise is slightly browned, about 10 minutes.

Nutritional Analysis: 578 calories, FAT 53 g, PROTEIN 11 g, CARB 13.5 g, FIBER 5 g, CHOL 54 mg, IRON 10 mg, SODIUM 599 mg, CALC 231 mg

Health Benefit
Popeye wins again. This recipe provides 170 percent of the RDA for vitamin A, 95 percent for vitamin C, and 51 percent for iron. And besides that? It tastes good and is easy to make.

Sautéed Salmon with Lavender
on a Bed of Summer Vegetables

Herbes de Provence, a perfume-y blend of herbs from the South of France containing rosemary, lavender, savory, and thyme, will lift a salmon fillet to new heights. Just marinate 15 minutes or so while you sauté the vegetables, and the result will be well worth your patience. The crisp, aromatic crust and a tender cooked-to-order fillet makes your mouth water. Don't want your fish rare? Cook it longer.

MAKES 2 SERVINGS

Preparation time: 20 minutes
Cooking time: 20 minutes

Two 6-ounce salmon fillets

1 tablespoon *herbes de Provence*

½ teaspoon kosher salt

½ teaspoon freshly milled black pepper

2 tablespoons olive oil

1 cup chopped red bell pepper

1 cup chopped green bell pepper

2 garlic cloves, minced

1 teaspoon finely chopped fresh flat-leaf
   parsley

1 cup chopped zucchini

Place the salmon on a sheet of wax paper. Rub the herbs, salt, and pepper into both sides; cover with plastic wrap and set aside. Preheat a large skillet over medium-high heat. Film it with 1 tablespoon of the oil. Add the peppers, garlic, parsley, and zucchini. Season to taste with salt and freshly milled black pepper. Sauté, stirring often, until golden brown and crisp-tender, 8 to 10 minutes. Remove to warmed dinner plates. Add the remaining tablespoon of oil to the pan and add the fish, skin side up. Pan-fry 5 to 8 minutes, turning only once. Lay fish atop the vegetables and serve.

Nutritional Analysis: 428 calories, FAT 25 g, PROTEIN 36 g, CARB 14 g, FIBER 5 g,
CHOL 94 mg, IRON 4 mg, SODIUM 663 mg, CALC 70 mg

Health Benefit

This one-dish dinner contains not only a big dose of omega-3s and vitamin A in the salmon, but also a generous serving of vitamins A and C in the peppers.

Five-Spice Salmon Over Spaghetti Squash with Cilantro

Five-spice powder, a piquant mixture of ground spices, can be found in the spice section of supermarkets and in Asian grocery stores. Though the spices vary from brand to brand, five-spice powder generally includes ground anise seed, star anise, cloves, cinnamon, and Szechuan peppercorns. Rub it onto chicken breasts, veal, pork chops, or fish to give those meats a kick in the pants. Use it sparingly; a little goes a long way.

Preparation time: 10 minutes
Cooking time: 10 minutes

MAKES 2 SERVINGS

½ teaspoon five-spice powder

1 teaspoon grated orange zest

½ teaspoon sugar

¼ teaspoon kosher salt

½ teaspoon freshly milled black pepper

Two 6-ounce salmon fillets

2 teaspoons Dijon mustard

1 tablespoon peanut oil

2 cups Roasted Spaghetti Squash (page 48)

2 tablespoons minced fresh cilantro

Stir together the five-spice powder with orange zest, sugar, salt, and pepper in a small bowl. Rub into both sides of the fillets on wax paper. Brush the mustard onto the fillets.

Heat a large skillet over medium-high heat, then film the bottom with the oil. Pan-fry the fillets, turning only once, until crisp and brown on the outside, 5 to 8 minutes total.

Meanwhile, divide the squash between two warmed dinner plates. Top with the fish fillets and garnish with the cilantro.

Nutritional Analysis: 352 calories, FAT 18 g, PROTEIN 35 g, CARB 10 g, FIBER 2 g, CHOL 94 mg, IRON 2 mg, SODIUM 505 mg, CALC 55 mg

Cooking Lesson

Spaghetti squash is a terrific vegetable to keep on hand in the refrigerator. It's practically carb-free, and offers crunch and that welcome mouth feel you used to get from pasta.

Poached Salmon on Leeks with *Herbes de Provence*

Perfume-y leeks and *herbes de Provence* will waft through your house when you make this classic poached-fish recipe. The pastel colors of the leeks under the coral pink salmon are pleasing to the eye.

MAKES 2 SERVINGS

Preparation time: 5 minutes

Cooking time: 15 minutes

4 cups (two 15½-ounce cans) low-sodium
   chicken broth
1 cup water
3 tablespoons *herbes de Provence*

1 medium leek, quartered and cleaned
   (see note)
Two 6-ounce salmon fillets
2 tablespoons unsalted butter
¼ cup heavy cream

In a large skillet with a tight-fitting lid, combine the chicken broth, water, and the *herbes de Provence*. Bring to a boil over high heat, cover, then reduce the heat to medium-low. Add the leeks and cook for 7 to 10 minutes. Place the salmon fillets on top of the leeks, skin side down, cover and cook for 4 to 5 minutes, or until the salmon is opaque. Using a slotted spoon or tongs, remove the salmon and leeks to a warm plate and cover. Add butter and cream to the pan and cook for 5 minutes reducing the sauce. Divide the sauce between two soup plates. Top with leeks, then salmon. Serve immediately.

Nutritional Analysis: 552 calories, FAT 37 g, PROTEIN 42 g, CARB 13 g, FIBER 3 g,
CHOL 173 mg, IRON 4 mg, SODIUM 431 mg, CALC 140 mg

Cooking Lesson

LEEKS are a little sandy and can be difficult to deal with. To quarter and clean a leek, trim off the roots as if you are trimming a beard, leaving a short "stubble" to hold the leek together. Then quarter the leek lengthwise; the quarters will be held together with the remaining roots. Carefully separate the layers of leek and wash between them. Put the layers back in place once you have washed them. Cut enough off the dark green top so that the leek will fit lengthwise in the pan.

Grilled Swordfish with Salsa

Grill this firm-fleshed fish over charcoal, on a gas grill, or in the kitchen in a ridged grill pan. The result is always a full-flavored, meaty fish. Add a dollop of your favorite salsa, and you're a Southwestern gourmet. Tune up commercial salsa with a handful of fresh cilantro, and it looks as if you studied in Santa Fe.

MAKES 2 SERVINGS

Preparation time: 10 minutes
Cooking time: 10 minutes

Two 6-ounce boneless, skinless swordfish steaks, ¾ inch thick
1 tablespoon olive oil
2 cups shredded iceberg lettuce
1 cup sliced radishes

1 Hass avocado
2 tablespoons best-quality salsa pumped up with a little fresh cilantro
Grated zest and juice of 1 lime

Preheat the gas, charcoal, or electric grill. Brush the fish with olive oil on both sides. Grill the fish, turning once after it has browned on the bottom (about 2 minutes), then finish on the second side, cooking until the fish is translucent in the middle (2 to 3 more minutes). Meanwhile, make a bed of lettuce, radishes, and avocado on two warmed dinner plates. Transfer the cooked fish to the dinner plates and top each steak with a big dollop of salsa. Squeeze lime juice over all and sprinkle with zest.

Nutritional Analysis: 387 calories, FAT 27 g, PROTEIN 26 g, CARB 12 g, FIBER 6 g, CHOL 45 mg, IRON 2 mg, SODIUM 175 mg, CALC 36 mg

Cooking Lesson

When buying prepared salsa, read the labels. Some of those in jars have big jolts of sugar lurking inside. Go for the fresh salsa in the refrigerator case. It's more likely to be made from pure tomatoes or other fruits and spicy accents.

Menu Suggestion

Watermelon for dessert will give your dinner the summery finish it deserves, and with no more than 5 carbs, provided you restrict yourself to a half cup or so.

Tuna Steaks with Tarragon Mayonnaise

Sushi-grade or yellowfin tuna is mild, meaty, and as satisfying as steak. Top it off with tasty tarragon mayonnaise you've stirred together, and it's a high-protein meal that satisfies. The naturally sweet flavor of squash makes a satisfying complement to the meaty tuna. Per serving it will add only 65 calories, 3.6 grams carbohydrate, and .7 grams protein.

Preparation time: 5 minutes
Cooking time: 6 minutes

MAKES 2 SERVINGS

2 teaspoons mayonnaise
2 tablespoons minced fresh or 2 teaspoons dried tarragon plus tarragon sprigs for garnish

Two 6-ounce tuna steaks, 1 inch thick
Salt and cracked pepper to taste
1 teaspoon olive oil
Squashed Winter Squash (recipe follows)

Stir together the mayo and tarragon in a small bowl. Cover and set aside. Heat a heavy skillet or ridged grill pan over medium-high heat. Pat the tuna dry with paper towels, then season to taste with salt and cracked pepper. Dab olive oil over the surfaces of the fish. Pan grill about 3 minutes per side for medium. Transfer to warmed dinner plates. Top each steak with a dollop of tarragon mayonnaise, and garnish with tarragon sprigs. Place a mound of squash beside the tuna.

Nutritional Analysis including the squash: 374 calories, FAT 19 g, PROTEIN 39 g, CARB 11 g, FIBER 3 g, CHOL 113 mg, IRON 3 mg, SODIUM 192 mg, CALC 86 mg

Cooking Lesson
Sushi-grade tuna means what it says. The fish is so fresh and of such good quality you could eat it raw. However, if the surface looks opaque white, don't worry. The meat color changes from sitting on the ice, but its quality is not affected.

Squashed Winter Squash

One ½-pound winter squash (butternut, hubbard)
2 tablespoons unsalted butter
Salt and freshly milled black pepper to taste

Prick the surface of the squash in several places with a fork. Place it in the microwave, and cook on high (100 percent power) until it's soft through, about 8 minutes. Alternatively, oven roast it at 400°F for about 45 minutes. Cut the squash in half, scoop out and discard the seeds, then scoop the flesh into a bowl. Add the butter and generous amounts of salt and pepper. Mash well.

Skewered Scallops with Prosciutto and Basil on a Bed of Creamed Spinach

Bundles of tender scallops enfolded in basil leaves and paper-thin slices of rosy prosciutto look as if you slaved away all day. You didn't. Present on a bed of creamed spinach, and you've made a fine dinner in less than half an hour. Serve the wrapped shellfish as a cocktail appetizer, too. Grill the scallop bundles on the barbecue, or cook them in a pan. Just take care not to over-cook them.

MAKES 2 SERVINGS

Preparation time: 10 minutes

Cooking time: 10 minutes

2 ounces thinly sliced prosciutto

12 large fresh basil leaves

12 ounces large sea scallops

CREAMED SPINACH

1 tablespoon olive oil

12 ounces fresh baby spinach

2 tablespoons cream

Salt to taste

½ teaspoon freshly milled black pepper

Pinch of freshly grated nutmeg

Soak 12 small wooden skewers in water for at least 20 minutes. Place a prosciutto slice on a work surface, then lay a basil leaf at one end. Top with a scallop. Wrap the prosciutto around the scallop and basil, tucking in the sides. Repeat the process to make 12 packets. Thread onto the soaked skewers, cover, and set them aside. Heat a grill or a large skillet.

Grill the packets over a medium charcoal fire or in the skillet, filmed with some of the olive oil, until the prosciutto begins to sizzle. Turn once and continue cooking, no more than 5 minutes total.

Meanwhile, sauté spinach in a large skillet with a little of the oil, just until wilted. Add the cream, season to taste with salt, pepper, and a little nutmeg. To serve, make a bed of creamed spinach on each of two warmed dinner plates. Slide the scallop packet off the skewers and arrange them on the spinach.

Nutritional Analysis: 339 calories, FAT 16 g, PROTEIN 40 g, CARB 11 g, FIBER 5 g, CHOL 88 mg, IRON 6 mg, SODIUM 696 mg, CALC 228 mg

Cooking Lesson

How to tell if charcoal is hot enough: When the charcoal is mostly coated with white ash, hold your hand a couple of inches above the grill and begin counting: "one-thousand-one, one-thousand-two, one-thousand-three," and so on. If you can only hold your hand for the 1,001 count, the fire is very hot. Up to 1,003 is medium-hot, and up to 1,005 is medium. If you can count any longer, your grill is not hot enough to cook.

Menu Suggestion

Finish this dinner with one of the newly available sugar-free desserts in the frozen desserts section of the supermarket—ice cream, Popsicles, cheesecakes—look for them. America's manufacturers are beginning to get it. We want dessert, but we don't want killer carbs.

Divers' Scallops and Leeks in a Bed of Ginger Cream

Nothing seems more luxurious than huge, tender scallops swimming in a spicy cream with pale, limp leeks adding their sweet note. Who would ever call this diet food?

Preparation time: 15 minutes

Cooking time: 8 to 10 minutes

MAKES 2 SERVINGS

12 ounces large sea scallops

1 tablespoon unsalted butter

2 medium leeks, quartered, cleaned, and all
    but 1 inch of green trimmed

2 tablespoons minced shallots

1 teaspoon dry vermouth

2 tablespoons minced fresh ginger

2 tablespoons heavy cream

1 cup low-sodium chicken broth

½ teaspoon freshly milled black pepper

Salt to taste

Pat the scallops with a paper towel. Heat the skillet over medium-high heat, then film the bottom with butter. Add scallops and cook without moving until golden on the edges, turning only once, 3 to 4 minutes. Remove to two warmed dinner plates and cover.

Add the leek and shallots, vermouth, ginger, heavy cream, and chicken broth to the skillet. Cook and stir until the mixture is thick, about 3 minutes. Taste and adjust seasonings with salt and pepper. Arrange the leeks beside the scallops on each plate and pour the sauce over all.

Nutritional Analysis: 298 calories, FAT 13 g, PROTEIN 31 g CARB 12 g, FIBER 1 g, CHOL 92 mg, IRON 2 mg, SODIUM 839 mg, CALC 82 mg

Cooking Lesson

What are divers' scallops? The best-quality hand-harvested scallops that come to only the best fish markets and restaurants. You can spot them because they're extra-large, and are not sitting in a tub of milky liquid. What does this mean? No preservative has been sprayed on them. Properly cooked scallops should be golden brown on the outside and fork tender. Leave them in the pan too long and they get dry and rubbery. Take care not to overcook them. If you paid top dollar for hand-harvested divers' scallops, you don't want to ruin them with careless handling.

Crabmeat Florentine with a Swiss Cheese Sauce

The marriage of sweet crabmeat with bitter spinach is moderated by this silky smooth Swiss Cheese Sauce. Add a glass of white wine for a perfect celebration meal.

MAKES 2 SERVINGS

Preparation time: 15 minutes

Cooking time: 20 minutes (concurrent)

3 tablespoons unsalted butter

2 tablespoons minced shallot

1 garlic clove, minced

1 cup sliced mushrooms

6 ounces fresh crabmeat, picked over for bits of shell and cartilage

1 tablespoon dry white wine

1 tablespoon heavy cream

12 ounces baby spinach

SWISS CHEESE SAUCE

1 teaspoon unsalted butter

1 teaspoon all-purpose flour

¾ cup milk

½ teaspoon kosher salt

½ teaspoon freshly milled black pepper

¼ teaspoon cayenne

¼ cup grated Swiss cheese

1 tablespoon pine nuts

Preheat the oven to 400°F. Generously butter two ramekins or scallop shells. Melt 2 tablespoons of the butter over medium heat in a large skillet, then add the shallot and garlic and cook until translucent, about 3 minutes. Add the mushrooms and cook 3 to 5 minutes more, then add the crabmeat, wine, and cream. Cook and stir until well combined, about 3 minutes, then transfer to a bowl. Heat the remaining tablespoon of butter in the skillet and add the spinach. Cook over high heat just until wilted, 1 or 2 minutes, then divide it between the two prepared ramekins. Top with the crab mixture.

Make the sauce by melting the 1 teaspoon of butter in the skillet or saucepan over medium heat. Add the flour and cook until it turns golden. Add the milk all at once, then add the salt and pepper, and cayenne. Cook over medium heat until thick. Remove from heat and stir in the cheese.

Pour the sauce evenly over the ramekins. Top with pine nuts. Pop them into the oven and cook until bubbly and brown, about 15 minutes.

Nutritional Analysis: 452 calories, FAT 30 g, PROTEIN 30 g, CARB 16 g, FIBER 5 g, CHOL 170 mg, IRON 6 mg, SODIUM 1,205 mg, CALC 520 mg

Cooking Lesson

Your ability to buy fresh crab used to depend upon your proximity to the crab pots, but nowadays cans of pasteurized fresh crab are sold at the fish counters of supermarkets from coast to coast. However, really *fresh* crab is still the much better alternative.

Curried Shrimp on Caramelized Onions

The bright colors, intense flavors, and varied textures of this recipe will make you forget that you are on a controlled regimen. Can food this rich really be diet food!?

MAKES 2 SERVINGS

Preparation time: 10 minutes

Cooking time: 10 minutes

Onion carmelizing time: 30 minutes (concurrent)

Carmelized Onions (recipe follows)

1 tablespoon unsalted butter

2 tablespoons olive oil

2 tablespoons chopped onions

1 teaspoon curry powder

½ teaspoon kosher salt

1 pound medium shrimp, peeled and deveined

1 tomato, finely chopped, plus minced tomato for garnish

¼ cup heavy cream

Toasted sliced almonds, for garnish

Cook the Caramelized Onions, following the directions opposite. When they have been in the oven for 15 minutes, begin the shrimp. Melt the butter and olive oil in a medium skillet over medium-high heat. Stir in the raw onions and cook until onions become golden, 3 to 5 minutes. Add the curry powder and salt and cook for 1 more minute. Toss in shrimp and cook just until they begin to turn pink, about 3 minutes. Add the chopped tomato and cream and cook for 1 more minute. Remove from the heat.

Divide the Caramelized Onions between two plates. Top with curried shrimp. Garnish with additional minced tomatoes and toasted almonds.

Nutritional Analysis, including Caramelized Onions: 528 calories, FAT 38 g, PROTEIN 37 g, CARB 9 g, FIBER 2 g, CHOL 394 mg, IRON 6 mg, SODIUM 1,651 mg, CALC 110 mg

Caramelized Onions

2 medium onions or 1 large Vidalia or Walla
Walla, thinly sliced
1 tablespoon unsalted butter

1 tablespoon olive oil
½ teaspoon salt
Freshly milled black pepper to taste

Preheat the oven to 400° F. Toss together the onions, butter, olive oil, salt, and pepper in a 13 × 9 × 2-inch pan. Spread the onions evenly across the bottom of the pan. Place in the oven, uncovered, for 30 minutes. Give the onions a stir about every 10 minutes. Ovens vary in heat, so keep an eye on them. They should be brown, not black.

Cooking Lesson

Curry powder must always be toasted or sautéed in fat to cook thoroughly before adding other ingredients. If you see a recipe that skips this step, it is a mistake. Flavor releases in the presence of heat and fat. You can toast curry powder easily in a dry skillet for 1 minute. We often toast curry powder in the toaster oven right on the baking sheet for the same amount of time it takes to toast a piece of toast.

Roasted Shrimp with Fresh Ginger on Wilted Watercress

The sweet flavor of shrimp is complemented by the complex blend known as five-spice powder, which is in turn counterbalanced by peppery watercress. A completely satisfying meal.

MAKES 2 SERVINGS

Preparation time: 5 minutes
Marinating time: 10 minutes
Cooking time: 7 minutes

2 tablespoons olive oil
1 tablespoon chopped fresh ginger
1 large garlic clove, finely chopped
¼ teaspoon five-spice powder
½ teaspoon kosher salt

½ teaspoon freshly milled black pepper
12 ounces large shrimp, peeled
4 cups watercress, rinsed and rough stems removed

Preheat the oven to 350°F. Stir together the oil, ginger, garlic, five-spice powder, salt, and pepper in a medium bowl. Toss in the shrimp, coating evenly, then cover and let stand for 10 minutes or so.

Arrange the shrimp in one layer on a baking sheet. Roast until the shrimp turns pink, 3 minutes. Remove the shrimp from the oven and set aside on a warm plate, covered, to keep warm. Place the watercress (still wet from washing) in a hot skillet and stir-fry just until wilted, about 1 minute. Divide the watercress between two dinner plates and top with hot roasted shrimp. Serve at once.

Nutritional Analysis: 263 calories, FAT 16 g, PROTEIN 28 g, CARB 3 g, FIBER 1 g, CHOL 242 mg, IRON 5 mg, SODIUM 888 mg, CALC 141 mg

Menu Suggestion

All we add to this all-in-one dinner is a clementine or tangerine on the side.

Health Benefit

Ginger has been prized in Asian cuisine for millennia, not only for its ability to boost flavors, but also for its help in promoting a long and peaceful life.

Spicy Freshwater Trout on a Bed of Peppery Watercress

What could be better than a freshwater trout, already deboned and ready for your skillet. Season it with surprising secret ingredients, including chili powder, curry, even pumpkin pie spice, then bake quickly and serve on a bed of peppery watercress.

MAKES 2 SERVINGS

Preparation time: 15 minutes

Cooking time: 8 to 10 minutes

1 tablespoon olive oil

12 ounces boned freshwater trout

¼ teaspoon kosher salt

½ teaspoon freshly milled black pepper

¼ cup bread crumbs

½ teaspoon curry powder

½ teaspoon chili powder

½ teaspoon pumpkin pie spice

⅛ teaspoon dried thyme

⅛ teaspoon cayenne

⅛ teaspoon ground nutmeg

**2 cups watercress, rinsed and tough stems
   removed**

Preheat the oven to 450° F. Film a baking dish with oil and add the fish, skin side down. In a small bowl, mix the salt, pepper, bread crumbs, curry powder, chili powder, pumpkin pie spice, thyme, cayenne, and nutmeg. Pat this mixture over the flesh of the fish. Drizzle the tablespoon of oil over all. Bake about 8 minutes, or until the fish flakes.

Meanwhile, divide watercress between two plates. Top with the fish and serve.

Nutritional Analysis: 363 calories, FAT 17 g, PROTEIN 39 g, CARB 12 g, FIBER 1 g,
CHOL 100 mg, IRON 2 mg, SODIUM 488 mg, CALC 196 mg

Cooking Lesson

Delicate whole trout that come deboned require careful handling. You can, of course, cook them in a skillet, but take care that you have a large enough spatula to turn them without breaking them up. A blast of hot air in the oven will cook them just as fast, and with no great risk of breakage. To transfer to a dinner plate, use one large or two medium spatulas, and carefully lift the fish to the dinner plate.

LAMB: THE PRINCE OF FLAVOR

Lamb is the most flavorful of all

the red meats. It is so sumptuous that grilled with just a little salt and pepper, it is heaven. Its distinct taste also makes it stand up nicely to bold flavors. It is a great way to fight food boredom. Because lamb is a very rich and dense food, you will often feel full on a smaller serving. Since we recommend monitoring your portions, lamb is great for dieters.

Interestingly, because sheep are easy to raise and will graze almost any-where, lamb is not mass-produced like beef, pork, and chicken (which com-promises their flavor). All of this grazing makes lamb develop a complex flavor and texture. Just think of the lamb you buy as "free range." Another interesting fact about lamb is how different one cut can taste from another. The shoulder is the most flavorful or gamy, great for stewing or roasting slowly. The rib chop is one of the milder cuts of lamb, and the loin chop is both flavorful and tender. The leg is closer to the shoulder in flavor, and because it is thick on one end and thin on the other, when it's grilled or roasted whole you can satisfy a range of desired levels of doneness—the thin part of the leg can be well-done, while the thicker part can be rare. Though at first glance lamb may seem expensive, because it is a very rich meat, a little goes a long way, so serving sizes of lamb are typically smaller than other types of meat. Get familiar with lamb; its distinctive flavor will bring new excitement to your table.

North African Spiced Lamb Chops
on a Bed of Mushrooms and Spinach

This classic mixture of North African spices plays nicely against the earthy/gamey flavor of lamb. Serve on a bed of sautéed mushrooms and spinach.

MAKES 2 SERVINGS

Preparation time: 5 minutes

Cooking time: 15 minutes

1 teaspoon coriander seeds

1 teaspoon ground cumin

2 teaspoons sweet paprika

½ teaspoon salt

1 tablespoon garlic powder

1 tablespoon olive oil

1 tablespoon water

4 lamb rib chops, frenched (see note)

Mushroom Spinach Sauté (recipe follows)

Mix together the coriander, cumin, paprika, salt, garlic powder, olive oil, and water to make a paste in a small bowl. Rub the spice paste on the lamb chops and let marinate for about 10 minutes.

Preheat a dry skillet over medium-high heat. Film with oil and add the chops. Sauté for medium-rare about 3 minutes, or longer for desired level of doneness. Arrange half of the Mushroom and Spinach mixture on each of two plates. Arrange the chops on top with the rib bones crossed.

Nutritional Analysis, including the spinach and mushrooms: 366 calories, FAT 21 g, PROTEIN 34 g, CARB 13 g, FIBER 5 g, CHOL 102 mg, IRON 7 mg, SODIUM 806 mg, CALC 158 mg

Mushroom Spinach Sauté

1 tablespoons unsalted butter

1 tablespoon olive oil

1 pint mushrooms, sliced

8 ounces baby spinach

While the lamb is marinating, melt the butter and olive oil in a medium skillet over medium-low heat. Add the mushrooms, cover, and cook over low heat for 10 minutes, stirring occasionally. Add the spinach, cover, and cook for another 3 minutes. The spinach will steam in the water left over from its washing and in the mushroom liquid.

Cooking Lesson

The rib chop is one of the mildest flavored cuts of lamb. To french a lamb rib chop, take a very sharp paring knife and scrape away all of the cartilage and film on the bone, leaving the bone perfectly clean, smooth, and dry. If you have a good butcher, you can ask him or her to french the rib chops for you. Butchers are happy, or at least willing, to perform this service. How do you know if the chops are cooked to suit you without cutting into the meat? Here's a chef's trick. Raw meat is soft. As it cooks, it firms up. Tap the top of the chop with your finger or the end of a wooden spoon. If it's as soft as the flesh between your thumb and forefinger of your relaxed hand, it's rare in the middle. If the meat is as firm up as that same spot on your hand when you have curled your fingers under to make a fist, the meat is medium. If the meat is as firm as the tip of your nose, it's well done.

Lamb Chops with Blueberry Vinegar Reduction

The blueberry vinegar reduction sauce is beautiful against the seared, medium-rare lamb. And the earthy flavor of the lamb against the sour flavor of the blueberries is fabulous.

MAKES 2 SERVINGS

Preparation time: 10 minutes

Cooking time: 12 minutes

2 tablespoons olive oil

Two 6-ounce lamb loin chops

2 garlic cloves, finely chopped

½ small tomato, minced

¼ cup blueberry or other fruit vinegar

¾ cup low-sodium chicken broth

½ cup heavy cream

½ cup fresh blueberries

Salt and freshly milled black pepper to taste

Heat the oil in a medium skillet over medium-high until almost smoking. Add the lamb chops and brown for about 3 minutes on each side. Remove from the heat and hold on a warm plate.

Add the garlic to the pan and sauté for 30 seconds or until fragrant. Add the tomato, vinegar, broth, and cream, and cook over medium heat until reduced by half, 3 to 5 minutes. Return the chops to the pan with any of their juices and cook, uncovered, for 3 more minutes. Add the blueberries and cook for 1 more minute. Taste and add salt and pepper to taste. Serve at once.

Nutritional Analysis: 575 calories, FAT 51 g, PROTEIN 18 g, CARB 11 g, FIBER 2 g, CHOL 146 mg, IRON 2 mg, SODIUM 1,034 mg, CALC 65 mg

Menu Suggestion
Serve with Roasted Asparagus with Lemon Curls (page 51). This will add about 4 carb grams and a wonderful variation in color.

Health Benefit
Blueberries, and in fact all berries, are a carb counter's best friend. They are low in sugar and high in flavor. And now they are shipped in from South America in the winter. They may cost a bit more, but what is your health worth?

Pan-Grilled Lamb Chops with a Cabernet Reduction and Pistachios

The bright green color of pistachios against the red sauce makes for a stunning dish with an interesting set of flavor variations. This dish is delicious with a purée of cauliflower.

MAKES 2 SERVINGS

Preparation time: 5 minutes

Cooking time: 15 minutes

1 cup beef broth

1 cup cabernet sauvignon or other dry red wine

2 tablespoons unsalted butter

Salt and freshly milled black pepper to taste

½ cup shelled pistachios, chopped

1 garlic clove, chopped

1 teaspoon ground black pepper

¼ cup finely chopped fresh flat-leaf parsley

Two 6-ounce loin lamb chops

1 tablespoon olive oil

¼ cup chopped fresh chives, for garnish

In a small saucepan, combine the broth and wine and bring to a simmer over medium heat. Reduce by a third or until the mixture is thick enough to coat the back of a spoon, about 4 minutes. Whisk in 1 tablespoon of the butter and salt and fresh pepper to taste. Keep warm.

Meanwhile, preheat a medium skillet over medium-high heat. Add the pistachios and toast in the dry skillet, until browned, about 1 minute. Add the remaining tablespoon of butter and the garlic and ground pepper and cook for 1 more minute. Add the parsley, stir, and remove the pistachio mixture to a small bowl; set it aside. Rub the lamb chops with the oil and reheat the skillet over medium-high heat. Add the chops and cook until the chops are brown, about 3 minutes per side or to desired level of doneness. Remove the skillet from the heat and brush the chops with a little of the reduction. Pool the remaining cabernet sauvignon reduction onto a plate and place a lamb chop on top. Spoon the pistachio mixture onto each chop, garnish with chives, and serve at once.

Nutritional Analysis: 671 calories, FAT 50 g, PROTEIN 27 g, CARB 12 g, FIBER 4 g, CHOL 99 mg, IRON 5 mg, SODIUM 1,246 mg, CALC 97 mg

Cooking Lesson

Almost all nuts and seeds are better if they are toasted first. This brings the oils of the nut to the surface and intensifies their flavor.

Cinnamon Lamb Sauté with Onion Tomato Sauce

Here's a dish that makes its own sauce right in the pan after you've cooked the chops for a satisfying, all-from-one-pan dinner.

Preparation time: 5 minutes

Cooking time: 25 minutes

MAKES 2 SERVINGS

Two 4- to 6-ounce chops about 1 inch thick
Salt and freshly milled black pepper to taste
1 teaspoon olive oil
½ cup chopped onion

2 garlic cloves, chopped
One 8–ounce can stewed tomatoes with their juices, chopped
1 teaspoon ground cinnamon

Season the chops with salt and pepper. Preheat a large sauté pan over medium-high heat, then film it with the olive oil. Brown them for a minute or two on each side, turning with tongs. Add the onions and garlic after you have turned the chops once—after about 4 minutes—and stir. To keep the onions from burning, add a teaspoon of water. Cook and stir until the chops are browned thoroughly and the onions are golden, 8 to 10 minutes.

Remove the chops to a warm, covered dish. Reduce the heat to medium and add the tomatoes and cinnamon to the sauté pan. Season to taste with salt and pepper. Continue to cook about 15 minutes, uncovered, adding a little water as needed to maintain a thick, saucelike consistency. Divide the sauce between two warmed dinner plates, top with the chops, and serve.

Nutritional Analysis: 480 calories, FAT 32 g, PROTEIN 35 g, CARB. 13 g, FIBER 3 g, CHOL 128 mg, IRON 4 mg, SODIUM 934 mg, CALC 101 mg

Menu Suggestion

An enormous green salad on the side, a 4-ounce glass of red wine, and for dessert, a 1-ounce wedge of your favorite cheese with berries or a melon wedge will add about 6 grams of carbohydrate and 7 grams of protein to make this a well-rounded meal.

Saffron-Flavored Lamb Stuffed in a Red Pepper

Red peppers make the perfect container for this subtly flavored lamb dish.

MAKES 2 SERVINGS

Preparation time: 5 minutes
Cooking time: 15 minutes

2 large red or yellow bell peppers

4 teaspoons unsalted butter

1 tablespoon plus 1 teaspoon dry vermouth

8 ounces ground lamb

2 tablespoons finely chopped lemon zest

1 tablespoon heavy cream

2 tablespoons grated Parmesan cheese

½ teaspoon saffron threads, soaked in
   1 tablespoon warm water

1 tablespoon finely chopped fresh flat-leaf
   parsley

1 large egg yolk

3 cups mesclun salad tossed in Mustard
   Vinaigrette (see page 130)

Heat the oven to 350° F. Slice off the top of each pepper, then core and clean it. Meanwhile, melt the butter with the vermouth in a large skillet over medium-low heat. Brush the insides of the peppers with some of the vermouth and butter mixture and set them aside. Add the ground lamb and lemon zest to the skillet and cook until the meat is well done, about 5 minutes. Remove from the heat and add the cream, Parmesan, saffron with water, and parsley. When the mixture is cool enough to touch comfortably (so as not to cook the egg), add the egg yolk.

Stuff the mixture into the peppers, place them in a baking pan, and bake for 30 minutes. Serve the stuffed peppers nestled in a bed of baby mesclun greens tossed with a light vinaigrette.

Nutritional Analysis: 535 calories, FAT 42 g, PROTEIN 34 g, CARB 7 g, FIBER 2 g,
CHOL 264 mg, IRON 3 mg, SODIUM 320 mg, CALC 154 mg

Honey-Mustard Lamb Chops on a Bed of Spaghetti Squash

Golden spaghetti squash is the perfect complement to this amber-colored sauce, and it is all complemented by the subtle taste of honey.

MAKES 2 SERVINGS

Preparation time: 5 minutes

Cooking time: 15 minutes

1 teaspoon honey

1 tablespoon grainy mustard

4 lamb loin chops, about 10 ounces

1 garlic clove, halved

1 teaspoon olive oil

1 teaspoon minced fresh rosemary

Freshly milled black pepper to taste

Cooking spray or vegetable oil

Rosemary sprigs for garnish

Roasted Spaghetti Squash (recipe follows)

Preheat the broiler. Stir the honey and mustard together in a small bowl and set aside. Rub the lamb chops with the garlic, olive oil, rosemary, and black pepper. Spray a skillet or indoor grill with cooking spray and cook the chops until golden, about 3 minutes per side. Remove the chops, baste with the honey mustard mixture, and finish cooking under the broiler for 3 more minutes, or until the chops have reached desired degree of doneness. Garnish them with rosemary sprigs and serve on a bed of Roasted Spaghetti Squash.

Nutritional Analysis, including the squash: 530 calories, FAT 36 g, PROTEIN 34 g, CARB 15 g, FIBER 3 g, CHOL 138 mg, IRON 3 mg, SODIUM 279 mg, CALC 76 mg

Roasted Spaghetti Squash

MAKES 4 TO 6 CUPS

1 spaghetti squash, about 2 pounds

2 teaspoons butter

Salt and freshly milled black pepper to taste

Preheat the oven to 450°F. Slice the spaghetti squash in half and place the halves on a cookie sheet, cut side down. Cook for 30 minutes. Hold the squash in an oven mit and scoop out the seeds, then, using a fork, scrape out the strands of squash into a bowl. Toss with butter, salt, and pepper.

Peppered Lamb Chops with Bitter Greens, Walnuts, and Cranberries

The spicy, crunchy crust on the outside of these chops is just the first of the flavor hits you'll get from this one-dish dinner: sweet, salty, bitter, and sour flavors, and hot besides, all rolled into one. Who could ask for anything more?

Preparation time: 20 minutes

Cooking time: 15 minutes

MAKES 2 SERVINGS

1 teaspoon olive oil

8 ounces thick loin lamb chops (2 to 4, depending upon the size)

1 garlic clove, cut in slivers

½ teaspoon cracked black peppercorns

4 cups mixed bitter greens, such as escarole, chicory, and/or radicchio, washed, dried, and torn

1 tablespoon chopped walnuts

1 tablespoon dried cranberries

DRESSING

1 tablespoon tarragon vinegar

1 tablespoon extra-virgin olive oil

1 tablespoon finely chopped shallots

1 teaspoon Dijon mustard

1 tablespoon water

½ teaspoon kosher salt

½ teaspoon freshly milled black pepper

Heat a large skillet over medium-high heat, then film it with the oil. While the pan is heating, make small incisions in the chops with a paring knife and insert slivers of garlic. Press the cracked peppercorns into the chops, then sauté, turning only once, until golden, 3 to 5 minutes per side.

While the chops cook, place salad greens in a large bowl along with the walnuts and dried cranberries. Whisk together the dressing ingredients in a small bowl, then toss with the salad. Divide the greens between two dinner plates, top with the sautéed chops, and serve.

Nutritional Analysis: 398 calories, FAT 28 g, PROTEIN 22 g, CARB 14 g, FIBER 8 g, CHOL 69 mg, IRON 3 mg, SODIUM 780 mg, CALC 213 mg

Cooking Lesson

Learn to read labels so you don't sabotage yourself at the grocery store. "Dried cranberries" are just that, but "craisins" or "crannies" have been processed with fruit juice and have enough sugar in them to add an unwanted dose of carbs.

Roast Lamb Chops on Asparagus Spears with Lemon and Garlic

Locate your 10-inch cast-iron (or ironclad) skillet, crank up the oven to blast-furnace temp, and you can make a fine one-dish dinner in which flavors caramelize into one intense experience.

Preparation time: 10 minutes

Cooking time: 20 minutes

MAKES 2 SERVINGS

Zest of 1 large lemon, removed in strips with a
   vegetable peeler, plus juice

2 garlic cloves, smashed

1 tablespoon dried rosemary

1 tablespoon olive oil

½ teaspoon kosher salt

8 ounces thick center-cut lamb loin chops

1 large lemon, cut into 6 thick slices

1 teaspoon chopped fresh chives

Roasted Asparagus (see opposite)

Preheat the oven to 450°F. Combine the lemon zest, garlic, rosemary, olive oil, and salt in a blender or food processor and pulse until finely chopped. Rub the mixture over the surface of the lamb chops. Film the bottom of a 10-inch skillet with olive oil, then cover with the lemon slices. Place the lamb chops on top and roast in the oven until cooked to the desired doneness, about 15 minutes for medium-rare. Adjust the seasonings with salt and pepper, sprinkle with chives, and serve. Serve glistening lamb chops alongside roasted asparagus on warm dinner plates.

Nutritional Analysis, including the asparagus: 456 calories, FAT 39 g, PROTEIN 18 g, CARB 10 g, FIBER 4 g, CHOL 66 mg, IRON 3 mg, SODIUM 636 mg, CALC 72 mg

Cooking Lesson

Since you have the oven on anyway, roast a vegetable to accompany the chops. Roasting concentrates foods' flavors and intensifies your dining pleasure. To roast vegetables, simply cut into uniform chunks, and arrange in a baking dish. Toss the vegetables with olive oil, season with salt and pepper, and pop them into the ultra-hot oven until they're crisp-tender, about 15 minutes for medium pieces (less for small pieces).

Roasted Asparagus with Lemon Curls

12 ounces asparagus

1 tablespoon olive oil

1 garlic clove, chopped

1 tablespoon lemon zest curls

Preheat the oven to 400° F. Snap off the bottoms of each asparagus spear where it breaks natu-rally and discard them. Place the spears in a bowl and toss with the olive oil, the chopped garlic, and lemon zest curls. Arrange them in the bottom of a well-greased glass baking dish. Roast in the oven for exactly 10 minutes. Remove and serve.

Menu Suggestion

Adding a side dish of roasted asparagus will only add only 4 grams of carbs. Go for a cheese course with this dinner to raise the protein grams to 27. Then it's perfect.

VEAL: THE DELICATE RED MEAT

Veal is a delicate and wonderful addition to any diet,

but few of us cook it at home. In fact, it only recently became widely available in supermarkets. Creamy pale and tender, veal is naturally low in fat and its mild flavor and winning texture make it very versatile. Veal, like poultry, is best cooked at medium to low temperatures to maximize moistness, flavor, and tenderness. However, because it is not as dense as beef, it cooks much faster. This is one reason why it is popular with chefs and with us in our quest to put dinner on the table in under 30 minutes. It also allows a cook to show off his or her ability to make a wonderful sauce.

Veal may seem costly, but given how quickly it cooks and what a compara-ble entree purchased from a restaurant would cost, it *is* a bargain. In fact, the cost per serving of preparing even the most expensive cut of veal is much lower than a fast-food hamburger or take-out Chinese food.

We encourage you to make veal part of your weekly menu plan. We have included a variety of recipes that use the cuts of veal that cook in the shortest amount of time. You can experiment and try these recipes with alternative cuts of veal. We think you will be pleased with the results. Most important, you will find that you don't have to be in a four-star restaurant to enjoy veal.

Veal Stew with Sage

This copper-colored stew will warm your heart and your stomach. The lemon zest brings up the flavors, and the sage adds a subtle earthiness. Try it; you will fall in love with sage.

MAKES 2 SERVINGS

Preparation time: 10 minutes
Cooking time: 20 minutes

10 ounces veal cutlets, pounded to ½ inch
    thick and cut into bite-size pieces
2 tablespoons olive oil
½ cup coarsely chopped onion
½ cup coarsely chopped celery
¼ cup coarsely chopped carrot
1 tablespoon finely chopped fresh sage
One 8-ounce can tomatoes, chopped, liquid
    reserved

½ cup dry white wine
2 cups low-sodium chicken broth
1 tablespoon butter
Salt and freshly milled black pepper to taste
½ teaspoon finely chopped lemon zest
Fresh sage leaves for garnish

Toss the veal in some of the olive oil. Film a large skillet with the remaining oil. Sauté the veal pieces in batches over medium-high heat, being careful not to crowd the pan. Cook them until lightly browned on both sides, about 1 to 2 minutes per side. Remove the veal to a warm plate and keep warm. Add the onion, celery, carrot, and sage to the pan and sauté for 5 minutes, until the onion becomes translucent. Add the tomatoes, white wine, and broth and deglaze, scraping up all of the brown bits from the bottom of the pan. Cook the sauce over medium-high heat until reduced by a third, about 5 minutes. Return the meat to the pan, swirl in the butter, then add the salt and pepper and lemon zest and cook for 5 more minutes. Serve garnished with whole sage leaves.

Nutritional Analysis: 421 calories, FAT 20 g, PROTEIN 34 g, CARB 15 g, FIBER 4 g,
CHOL 141 mg, IRON 3 mg, SODIUM 720 mg, CALC 108 mg

Veal Meatballs in Port Sauce Over Caramelized Onions

Ground veal is inexpensive and delicate. If your butcher won't grind it for you, use your food processor to chop it finely. These tender, delicate meatballs are wonderful when served over Caramelized Onions. See page 37 for a foolproof way to caramelize onions, which we learned from a French chef.

Preparation time: 5 minutes
Cooking time: 25 minutes

MAKES 2 SERVINGS

10 ounces ground veal	**2 shallots, finely chopped**
1 large egg	**1 celery stalk, finely chopped**
1 tablespoon Dijon mustard	**2 cups low-sodium chicken broth**
¼ cup freshly grated Parmesan cheese	**¼ cup port wine**
1 tablespoon vegetable oil	**Caramelized Onions (page 37)**
1 teaspoon butter	

Thoroughly mix the veal, egg, mustard, and Parmesan by hand in a large bowl. Form into 2-inch meatballs with wet hands. Preheat a large skillet over medium-high heat. Add the oil and butter and heat until very hot, about 1 more minute. Add the meatballs and sauté until browned all over, about 5 minutes. Remove from the heat and transfer to a warm plate. Add the shallots and celery to the pan and sauté on medium heat for 3 minutes. Add the chicken broth and the port wine to deglaze the pan, scraping up all of the brown bits from the bottom. Return the meatballs to the skillet, including all of the liquid that has accumulated on the plate. Cook until cooked through, 5 to 10 more minutes. Serve over a bed of Caramelized Onions.

Nutritional Analysis, including Caramelized Onions: 467 calories, FAT 31 g, PROTEIN 33 g, CARB 7 g, FIBER 1 g, CHOL 148 mg, IRON 2 mg, SODIUM 626 mg, CALC 219 mg

Veal Cutlets in a Raspberry Balsamic Vinegar Sauce

The distinct flavor of balsamic vinegar against the sweetness of raspberries brings new zest to mild-flavored veal cutlets.

MAKES 2 SERVINGS

Preparation time: 10 minutes

Cooking time: 12 minutes

10 ounces veal cutlets, pounded to ¼ inch thick

2 tablespoons olive oil

2 garlic cloves, finely chopped

½ small tomato, cut in small dice

¼ cup balsamic vinegar

¾ cup low-sodium chicken broth

¼ cup heavy cream

½ cup raspberries (fresh or frozen)

Salt and freshly milled black pepper to taste

Toss the veal cutlets with 1 tablespoon of the olive oil. Heat the other tablespoon of oil in a medium skillet over medium-high heat. Add the veal cutlets and brown on each side, about 2 minutes per side. Remove from the heat and hold on a warm plate. Add the garlic and sauté until golden, about 30 seconds. Add tomato, vinegar, broth, and cream and boil until reduced by half, 3 to 5 minutes. Return the cutlets to the pan with any juices that have accumulated on the plate and cook for 3 more minutes. Add the raspberries and cook for 1 more minute. Season to taste with salt and pepper. Serve at once.

Nutritional Analysis: 530 calories, FAT 39 g, PROTEIN 33 g, CARB 12 g, FIBER 3 g, CHOL 164 mg, IRON 2 mg, SODIUM 720 mg, CALC 61 mg

Cooking Lesson

Using vinegar in a sauce, or in anything for that matter, is an old chef's trick for bringing out flavors. That is because the acid in vinegar makes your taste buds stand up and pay attention. So if you are cooking anything, especially with fruit or vegetables, and it tastes bland, try adding a dash of vinegar or citrus juice. Improving the flavor of everything you eat is key when you are restricting your diet.

Menu Suggestion

Serve with Cauliflower Purée (page 164). This will add about 5 grams of carbs and is a wonderfully subtle background for the flavorful sauce.

Veal Chops with Garlic and Rosemary and Eggplant and Red Pepper Purée

Veal chops and the piney flavor of rosemary are a nifty match for coppery-colored eggplant and red pepper purée.

MAKES 2 SERVINGS

Preparation time: 5 minutes

Cooking time: 10 minutes

Two 1-inch thick veal chops

1 teaspoon olive oil

2 garlic cloves, finely chopped

2 teaspoons minced fresh rosemary

Freshly milled black pepper to taste

Cooking spray or vegetable oil

Eggplant and Red Pepper Purée (page 167)

Rosemary sprigs for garnish

Rub the veal chops with the olive oil, garlic, rosemary, and black pepper. Spray a skillet or indoor grill with cooking spray and cook the chops over medium high heat for about 4–5 minutes per side. Spoon some of the Eggplant Red Pepper Purée onto each of two plates, top with a veal chop, and garnish with the rosemary sprigs.

Nutritional Analysis: 351 calories, FAT 18 g, PROTEIN 43 g, CARB 2 g, FIBER 2 g, CHOL 139 mg, IRON 2 mg, SODIUM 102 mg, CALC 38 mg

BEEF: OUR ALL-TIME FAVORITE

We do love beef.

We are from Texas and, in fact, from cattle people. That is to say, our grandfathers, great-grandfathers, and great-great-grandfathers were ranchers who raised cattle in the panhandle of Texas near Amarillo and Kansas long before technology made possible the deep-water wells that allowed that dry part of the world to be farmed. Despite what you might think, beef is still the most consumed meat in America, and its popularity is on the rise.

The fact is, beef is healthy. It provides an important combination of nutrients (zinc, iron, and protein) not present in such high concentrations in other foods. Today's ranchers are raising leaner and leaner beef that is a great source of protein. Besides, it just tastes good.

The beef people have recently marketed freshly cooked pot roasts that are ready in twelve minutes from your microwave. They're not bad for an emergency dinner, and we find these pot roasts to be great jump starts to more sophisticated dishes as well.

Beef has a distinct flavor that can stand up to many bold seasonings, but is good with just a little salt and pepper. The less expensive cuts add body to stews, and the more expensive ones are ready in minutes. They are still our favorites because of the convenience factor. And let's face it. If comfort food is the food trend that will be left standing in the next millennium, what could be more comforting than beef?

Sautéed Beef and Tomatoes with Whiskey and Black Bean Sauce

It's worth a trip to an Asian market to find dried, salted black beans, but if you can't locate them, the ready-made sauce makes a handy substitute. You'll see Chinese-style black bean garlic sauce in most supermarkets. If you buy the dried beans, they will last for years, sealed, in your pantry.

Preparation time: 20 minutes
Cooking time: 15 minutes

MAKES 2 SERVINGS

MARINADE

1 teaspoon kosher salt

2 teaspoons soy sauce

1 teaspoon whiskey (Scotch, Bourbon, Irish, or Canadian)

1 teaspoon cornstarch

2 teaspoons peanut oil

8 ounces lean flank steak, thinly sliced across the grain

1 tablespoon dried, salted black beans, or 2 tablespoons Chinese black bean garlic sauce

2 garlic cloves, crushed

2 tablespoons water

Scant tablespoon plus 1 teaspoon peanut oil

1 scallion, white and green parts, minced

4 medium plum tomatoes, cored and quartered

½ teaspoon sugar

½ cup low-sodium chicken broth

2 teaspoons oyster sauce

2 cups mixed bitter greens, such as escarole, chicory, or arugula, washed and spun dry

Combine the marinade ingredients in a medium bowl. Add the steak and rub the mixture into the meat with your fingers. Cover and set aside to marinate about 20 minutes. Meanwhile, mash the black beans and garlic together, and stir in water. Set aside.

Heat a large skillet over medium-high heat and add the scant tablespoon of peanut oil. Add the scallion and cook, stirring about 30 seconds. Add black bean and garlic mixture and cook 15 seconds, then add the meat and sauté until it begins to lose its pink color, 3 to 5 minutes. Transfer the meat to a bowl and set it aside.

Add the remaining teaspoon of oil to the pan and reheat, then add tomatoes. Sauté just until they begin to lose their shape, sprinkling sugar over them to hasten browning. Add the broth and cover. Cook until the tomatoes are thickened, about 2 minutes. Return the meat to the pan, add the oyster sauce, and sauté 1 additional minute.

Divide the greens between two plates and top with the beef and tomato sauté. Serve at once.

Nutritional Analysis: 310 calories, FAT 15 g, PROTEIN 28 g, CARB 13, FIBER 2 g, CHOL 58 mg, IRON 4 mg, SODIUM 1,440 mg, CALC 49 mg

Menu Suggestion

For an East-meets-West ending to this Asian-inspired meal, offer flavorful cheeses for dessert. Europeans don't require bread with their cheese, and if you select full-flavored varieties, you won't either. Try Explorateur, Cambozola, Gruyère, English Cheddar, or Parmiagiano-Reggiano. Offer slivers and some other nibbles—so satisfying. Thin slices of apple or pear make terrific backers.

Health Benefit

Cooked tomato is a good source of the antioxidant lycopene, which is more easily absorbed by the body when combined with fat, such as the peanut oil in this recipe.

Rosemary Beef Medallions with Red Pepper Sauce on a Bed of Mesclun

The intense flavors of rosemary and red pepper are just right with the earthy flavor of steak. Served over a bed of mesclun, this one dish makes a complete meal.

Preparation time: 15 minutes

Cooking time: 10 minutes

MAKES 2 SERVINGS

2 tablespoons butter

¼ cup fresh lime juice

1 teaspoon dried rosemary, crushed

¼ cup roasted red bell peppers, drained well
   and chopped (page 22)

Pinch of cayenne, to taste

Salt to taste

1 teaspoon olive oil

10 ounces beef tenderloin cut into
   ½-inch-thick rounds

2 cups mesclun or baby greens

In the bowl of a food processor with the blade removed, melt the butter in the microwave on high (100 percent power) for 30 seconds. Remove from the microwave, replace the metal blade in the food processor bowl and add the lime juice, rosemary, roasted red pepper, cayenne, and salt. Pulse the mixture until thoroughly mixed. Taste and adjust the seasoning and set aside.

Heat a large dry skillet. Film with the oil, add the beef medallions, and sauté until golden, for 5 minutes per side for medium-rare. Spoon the sauce onto two plates, arrange the meat in the pools of sauce, and add a pile of mesclun salad to the side. Serve at once.

Nutritional Analysis: 484 calories, FAT 28 g, PROTEIN 49 g, CARB 6 g, FIBER 2 g, CHOL 173 mg, IRON 7 mg, SODIUM 280 mg, CALC 55 mg

Health Benefit

The key to staying on a diet is being satisfied both in terms of feeling full and of not being bored by the same old flavors. Rosemary is a great secret weapon against "dinner boredom," it complements a host of other foods. It is such a strong flavor, you can overdo it with rosemary, so easy does it. Try rosemary with chicken, lamb, and olives.

Teriyaki-Rosemary Flank Steak Served on a Bed of Vinegared Bean Sprouts

One of the most interesting trends to emerge from the restaurant world is the layering of flavors, textures, and temperatures. This meal represents the concept well. The sweet flavor of the teriyaki juxtaposed with the pine-y flavor of rosemary is an inspired contrast. And the effect of serving the flavor-infused warm steak on a bed of crunchy, cold bean sprouts is quite satisfying.

Preparation time: 15 minutes
Marinating time: 5 to 10 minutes
Cooking time: 10 minutes

MAKES 2 SERVINGS

MARINADE

2 tablespoon teriyaki sauce

1 teaspoon soy sauce

¼ cup chopped onion

2 teaspoons orange juice

1 teaspoon dried rosemary, crushed

1 tablespoon sesame oil

1 garlic clove, crushed

Pinch of red pepper flakes

½ teaspoon salt

BEAN SPROUT BED

1 cup bean sprouts

2 tablespoons rice wine vinegar

1 teaspoon vegetable oil

1 teaspoon sesame oil

Pinch red pepper flakes

Salt to taste

1 teaspoon peanut oil

Fresh rosemary for garnish

8 ounces flank steak, thinly sliced across the grain

Combine the marinade ingredients in a medium bowl. Toss in the flank steak strips and coat each piece of meat thoroughly. Set aside for 5 to 10 minutes.

Toss together the ingredients for the bean sprout bed in a separate bowl. Set aside.

Preheat a dry wok over high heat for 3 minutes. Add the peanut oil and continue heating for 1 more minute. Add the flank steak in small batches and cook each batch until medium rare, 3 to 5 minutes, or to desired level of doneness. Divide sprouts between two plates and top with meat. Garnish with fresh rosemary and serve at once.

Nutritional Analysis: 401 calories, FAT 26 g, PROTEIN 34 g, CARB 10 g, FIBER 2 g, CHOL 76 mg, IRON 4 mg, SODIUM 850 mg, CALC 65 mg

Grilled New York Strip and Portobello on Watercress and Bean Sprouts

Pour yourself a glass of good red wine, say a pinot noir from Oregon. The fruity pinot flavor is a great foil for the blue cheese and steak and works well with the salad. All you need is candle-light and your best friend.

Preparation time: 15 minutes

Cooking time: 5 to 8 minutes

MAKES 2 SERVINGS

One 10-ounce New York strip steak

½ teaspoon kosher salt

½ teaspoon cracked black pepper

1 large portobello mushroom cap, sliced

1 tablespoon olive oil

1 ounce Stilton cheese, cut into thin slivers

4 cups watercress, rinsed and thick stems removed

1 cup bean sprouts

2 cherry tomatoes

VINAIGRETTE

1 tablespoon sherry vinegar

1 tablespoon grainy mustard

1 teaspoon Dijon mustard

2 tablespoons extra-virgin olive oil

½ teaspoon kosher salt

½ teaspoon freshly milled black pepper

Preheat a skillet or ridged grill pan. Meanwhile, pat the steaks dry with paper towels and season lightly with salt and pepper. Brush the portobellos lightly with olive oil. Pan grill the steak and mushrooms together, about 5 minutes per side for medium-rare, turning only once. When the steak is just done, top with Stilton slices.

While the steak and mushroom are cooking, toss the watercress and bean sprouts together and compose on two large dinner plates. Whisk together the vinaigrette ingredients, then drizzle over the salad. Cut the steak in two pieces and divide between the plates, along with the grilled portobello slices.

Nutritional Analysis: 575 calories, FAT 39 g, PROTEIN 48 g, CARB 8 g, FIBER 3 g, CHOL 119 mg, IRON 5 mg, SODIUM 1,669 mg, CALC 164 mg

Cooking Lesson

You needn't eat an enormous 12-ounce steak to get the nutrition you need. A piece of lean meat about the size of the palm of your hand will weigh out at about 4 ounces before you cook it, and that constitutes a healthy serving.

Kalamata-Crusted New York Strip on a Bed of Arugula

Use a restaurant technique to deliver maximum punch to the quintessential steak. This means giving it a quick sear on the stovetop and then transferring it to the oven to finish cooking. This technique is less stressful for cooks who have lots going on all at once. Is this you?

Preparation time: 15 minutes
Cooking time: 10 minutes

MAKES 2 SERVINGS

One 12-ounce New York strip steak
$\frac{1}{2}$ teaspoon kosher salt or to taste
$\frac{1}{2}$ teaspoon freshly milled black pepper or to
  taste

$\frac{1}{2}$ cup pitted kalamata olives
2 teaspoons extra-virgin olive oil
4 cups arugula
1 teaspoon balsamic vinegar

Preheat the oven to 400°F. Pat the steak dry and season it with the salt and pepper. Purée the olives in a food processor. Heat an ovenproof skillet over high heat, then film it with oil. Sear the steak 2 to 4 minutes per side. Right after you have turned it once, top the steak with the olive paste. Place the skillet in the hot oven and cook 5 to 7 minutes for rare or medium-rare. Transfer to a cutting board and let the meat rest 3 to 4 minutes, then cut on the diagonal into thin slices.

While the meat is resting, divide the arugula between two plates. Whisk together the oil and vinegar, then drizzle over the arugula. To serve, fan the meat on top of the arugula.

Nutritional Analysis: 456 calories, FAT 25 g, PROTEIN 50 g, CARB 8 g, FIBER 4 g,
CHOL 129 mg. IRON 6 mg, SODIUM 1,030 mg, CALC 100 mg

Cooking Lesson

Nothing delivers protein more purely than red meat. You get protein plus a big dose of essential B vitamins, iron, and zinc, especially important for women and growing children.

Filet Mignon Caesar

What a trend Caesar Cardini started in Border Mexico during the Roaring Twenties. Caesar salads have attained a permanent place in American cuisine. Here we gild the lily with buttery filet. Hold the croutons (obviously).

Preparation time: 15 minutes

Cooking time: 10 to 15 minutes

MAKES 2 SERVINGS

2 hearts of romaine

DRESSING

1 garlic clove

½ teaspoon kosher salt

1 teaspoon anchovy paste

Grated zest from ½ lemon plus 1 teaspoon
    lemon juice

½ teaspoon Dijon mustard

3 drops Tabasco sauce

1 large egg, boiled for 1 minute

2 tablespoons olive oil

1 tablespoon freshly grated Parmesan cheese

Two 6-ounce filet mignons, each wrapped in a
    strip of bacon

½ teaspoon kosher salt

½ teaspoon freshly milled black pepper

Tear the hearts of romaine into bite-size pieces. Rub the inside of a wooden salad bowl with the garlic clove and salt. Add the anchovy paste, lemon juice, mustard, and Tabasco. Whisk the mixture, then break the egg into the bowl and whisk it in. Drizzle in the oil, whisking constantly, until emulsified. Add the Parmesan cheese and toss the greens into the dressing. Set aside.

Pat the steaks dry with paper towels. Season lightly with salt and pepper. Heat an indoor or outdoor grill, or a sauté pan over medium-high heat. Cook the steaks to desired doneness, 4 to 6 minutes per side for medium-rare. (See page 43 for instructions on determining doneness.) Keep warm.

To serve, divide the salad between two dinner plates and add a sizzling hot fillet.

Nutritional Analysis: 601 calories, FAT 42 g, PROTEIN 51 g, CARB 2 g, FIBER .5 g, CHOL 254 mg, IRON 7 mg, SODIUM 1,470 mg, CALC 83 mg

Hoisin Flank Steak on a Bed of Braised Bok Choy

Bright green bok choy leaves, tenderly cooked in chicken broth, make a perfect bed for glistening, golden brown flank steak, fanned out to reveal its medium-rare pink center.

Preparation time: 20 minutes

Cooking time: 20 minutes (concurrent)

MAKES 2 SERVINGS

12 ounces flank steak

2 tablespoons hoisin sauce

Grated zest from ½ orange plus 1 tablespoon
   fresh orange juice

1 tablespoon dry sherry

½ tablespoon grated fresh ginger

1 teaspoon Dijon mustard

¼ teaspoon sugar

1 teaspoon dark sesame oil

½ teaspoon freshly milled black pepper

1 tablespoon peanut oil

6 cups bok choy leaves

½ cup low-sodium chicken broth

Place the steak in a glass dish. Stir the hoisin, orange juice and zest, sherry, grated ginger, mustard, sugar, sesame oil, and pepper in a small bowl. Pour over the meat, cover, and set aside for at least 10 minutes and up to overnight (in the refrigerator).

Preheat a grill or large sauté pan. Add half the peanut oil to the pan or dab it on the meat if grilling. Cook the steak until medium-rare, basting often with marinade, 6 to 8 minutes per side. Let it stand a few moments, then cut into diagonal slices against the grain.

While the meat is cooking, heat a large skillet over medium-high heat. Wash the bok choy and add it to the pan with water clinging to the leaves. Stir-fry a few moments, then add the chicken broth. Cover, reduce the heat, and cook until tender, 5 to 8 minutes.

To serve, make beds of bok choy on two dinner plates and fan the meat on top.

Nutritional Analysis: 502 calories, FAT 28 g, PROTEIN 48 g, CARB 11 g, FIBER 1 g,
CHOL 116 mg, IRON 5 mg, SODIUM 741 mg, CALC 69 mg

Health Benefit

Making a bed of greens under a nutrient-dense lean steak gives you the best of all possible worlds. Not only do you get a big hit of protein, zinc, iron, and vitamin B from the meat, you'll also add a huge jolt of vitamin C from the greens.

Thai Style Beef Mint Salad

This dazzling green salad is truly mouthwatering. It combines salty, sour, and sweet flavors for a completely satisfying meal. The dressing recipe is a basic Thai sauce that can be used on many other mixed greens, bean sprouts, and cabbage. Some theorize that crunchy food is so appealing because it allows us to vent our frustrations; better to crunch on a salad than on potato chips . . . or your coworkers or your partner.

MAKES 2 SERVINGS

Preparation time: 20 minutes

Cooking time: 8 minutes for the steak
7 minutes for the eggs
(can be cooked
concurrently)

DRESSING

½ cup fresh lime juice (about 2 limes)

2 tablespoons fish sauce (nuoc mam)

¼ teaspoon sugar

2 teaspoons vegetable oil

One 6-inch piece fresh lemongrass (tender center cut into three 2-inch pieces)

One 10-ounce New York strip steak

1 tablespoon chili powder (we love Gebhardt's)

2 cups romaine lettuce, washed, dried, and sliced into 1-inch-thick ribbons

¾ cup fresh mint leaves, cut into ribbons

½ cup fresh basil leaves, cut into ribbons

1 large hard-cooked egg, sliced

Mix together the dressing ingredients in a large salad bowl and set aside.

Heat an indoor or outdoor gas grill or a dry cast-iron skillet for 5 minutes, or light a charcoal fire. Grill the steak until medium-rare, 3 to 4 minutes on each side (if using a black skillet, you will want to spray it with cooking spray). When the meat is cooked, cut it into thin slices and toss with the dressing. Remove to a plate and sprinkle the steak slices with chili powder. Remove the lemongrass stalks from the dressing. Now, in the same bowl, toss in the romaine lettuce, mint leaves, and basil leaves. Toss the greens thoroughly and divide them equally between two plates. Top with slices of steak and sliced eggs. Sprinkle the eggs with chili powder.

Nutritional Analysis: 573 calories, FAT 33 g, PROTEIN 57 g, CARB 11 g, FIBER 3 g, CHOL 246 mg, IRON 7 mg, SODIUM 1,549 mg, CALC 133 mg

Cooking Lesson

Get aquainted with the Asian markets in your area. With the large influx of Asian immigrants to this country, nearly all communities have such a market. They traditionally carry Chinese, Japanese, and Southeast Asian ingredients. The prices are usually lower than what you will find at your primary grocery store. We have always found that if you ask the clerk to recommend a brand, you can learn a great deal about these exotic ingredients. Asian ingredients add lots of flavor with few calories.

Sesame Sirloin Salad

For maximum flavor and tenderness, buy the highest quality sirloin you see; *prime* is best. Take care to preheat the skillet thoroughly, film it with oil, then place the meat in serving side down. Don't move it until you're ready to turn it, and turn it only once.

MAKES 2 SERVINGS

Preparation time: 20 minutes
Cooking time: 10 minutes

2 teaspoons olive oil

8 ounces top sirloin, 1 inch thick

1 teaspoon freshly milled black pepper

Kosher salt

8 scallions, white part with about 1 inch of green part, cut in 2-inch pieces

1 red bell pepper, cored, seeded, cut in half lengthwise, sliced into ribbons

4 cups salad greens, washed, dried, and torn (radicchio, watercress, and/or escarole)

DRESSING

1 tablespoon soy sauce

1 tablespoon red wine vinegar

1 teaspoon sesame oil

1 teaspoon finely shredded fresh ginger

½ teaspoon kosher salt

Heat a large skillet over medium-high heat, then film it with the olive oil. Meanwhile, press pepper into both sides of the meat. Season lightly with kosher salt.

Place the meat, scallions, and red pepper in the hot skillet and cook until the vegetables begin to brown (turning as needed) and the steak is medium-rare, about 10 minutes total (3 to 4 minutes per side for the steak). Transfer the cooked meat and vegetables to a cutting board and let it stand about 5 minutes before cutting.

Whisk the dressing ingredients in a salad bowl. Add the greens and toss with the dressing. Divide between two large dinner plates.

Cut the meat against the grain into very thin slices. Fan the meat over the salad greens and arrange the scallions and peppers alongside.

Nutritional Analysis: 349 calories, FAT 16 g, PROTEIN 38 g, CARB 13 g, FIBER 5 g, CHOL 101 mg, IRON 6 mg. SODIUM 1,910 mg, CALC 101 mg

Menu Suggestion

Here's an ideal dinner to which you can add your favorite dessert. How about ½ cup of raspberries with 2 tablespoons of whipped cream? You'll add only 130 calories and 7 additional grams of carbohydrates.

PORK: MORE THAN JUST THE OTHER WHITE MEAT

Pork has a distinctly sweet flavor that marries well with many sauces and vegetables. In response to consumer concerns about fat levels, pork is now being bred to be leaner and leaner—much to the chagrin of senior culinary authorities, including Julia Child and Jaques Pepin, who lament that lean pork has less flavor.

Lean pork chops and tenderloin must be cooked quickly, lest they become too dry. However, pork responds well to fast cooking and, when properly handled, makes a succulent meal.

One of the old myths about pork is the fear of trichinosis. The fact is, there hasn't been a case of trichinosis in the United States in more than fifty years.

Pork breeders are extremely aware of this lingering fear and have addressed the food safety issues to the fullest. Besides, trichinae, the evil parasite that causes the dreaded trichinosis, is killed at 137°F. We recommend cooking pork until it is medium-rare, around 150°F; if you are a sissy, cook it to well done, 170°F. But in our opinion, pork is best left just slightly pink.

Sweet and satisfying, pork is the base of many of the world's finest cuisines, including Cantonese, French, Cajun, Southern, and Mexican. It adds flavor to a dish and blends well with other ingredients. From hot and spicy to subtle, pork adds a wonderful dimension to a high-protein menu in the fight against food boredom.

Pork Tenderloins with Orange Sections and Brussels Sprout Strips

Melding the sweetness of oranges with the bitter flavor of Brussels sprouts is a winning combination. Never fear if you think you hate Brussels sprouts. This method of cooking them brings out their hidden sweetness. Your view of them as just "baby cabbages" will be altered forever.

Preparation time: 10 minutes
Cooking time: 20 minutes

MAKES 2 SERVINGS

8 ounces pork tenderloin, sliced into ½-inch
   rounds
2 tablespoons vegetable oil
Salt and freshly milled black pepper
¼ cup finely chopped scallions
¼ cup port wine or medium red wine
1 cup low-sodium chicken broth

1 teaspoon tomato paste
¼ cup chopped orange sections
2 tablespoons grated orange zest
2 tablespoons unsalted butter
Brussels Sprouts Chiffonade with Cumin
   (see opposite)

Slice or pound each pork round between sheets of wax paper until ¼ inch thick. Toss the pork rounds in some of the cooking oil. Salt and pepper generously and set aside on a plate. Heat a dry skillet for 2 minutes over medium-high heat. Add the remaining oil and heat for 1 minute. Add the pork rounds and sauté until lightly browned, 1 to 2 minutes on each side. Remove the pork rounds from the pan and place on a warm plate.

Add the scallions to the skillet and cook for 30 seconds. Add the wine, broth, and tomato paste and deglaze the pan, scraping up all of the brown bits that stick to the bottom of the pan. Cook over medium heat for 3 minutes. Stir in the orange sections and orange zest and the butter and return the pork rounds to the sauce with any juices that have accumulated on the plate. Cook for 3 more minutes. Divide the sprouts equally onto two plates. Spoon the pork medallion sauce to the side of the sprouts. Lay the medallions in the sauce, just overlapping the Brussels sprouts. Serve at once.

Nutritional Analysis, including Brussels sprouts: 555 calories, FAT 40 g, PROTEIN 26 g, CARB 15 g, FIBER 4 g, CHOL 108 mg, IRON 3 mg, SODIUM 1,381 mg, CALC 69 mg

Brussels Sprouts Chiffonade with Cumin

2 tablespoons unsalted butter
1 cup Brussels sprouts, sliced into chiffonade (some will fall apart; don't worry about it)
½ cup chopped onion
¼ teaspoon ground cumin
¼ cup low-sodium chicken broth

Melt the butter over high heat in a large skillet. Stir in the Brussels sprout slices, onion, and cumin and sauté until slightly browned, 3 to 5 minutes. Add the chicken broth, reduce the heat to medium, cover, and cook for 3 more minutes.

Hoisin-Marinated Pork Chops on a Bed of Jicama and Red Cabbage Salad

Though one might assume that hoisin is verboten this recipe demonstrates well our mantra "all things in moderation." Used carefully, hoisin adds a rich flavor note to the pork. Cook this on an outdoor grill if you wish.

MAKES 2 SERVINGS

Preparation time: 10 minutes
Cooking time: 20 minutes

2 teaspoons hoisin sauce

2 teaspoons rice wine vinegar

2 tablespoons soy sauce

1 teaspoon garlic powder

1 teaspoon sesame oil

Two 6-ounce thick-cut pork chops, bone in

Salt and freshly milled black pepper to taste

1 teaspoon vegetable oil

Jicama and Red Cabbage Salad (see opposite)

1 scallion, including green part, minced, for garnish

1 tablespoon toasted sesame seeds for garnish

Combine the hoisin, vinegar, soy sauce, garlic powder, and sesame oil in a shallow baking dish. Add the pork chops, turning them a few times to coat thoroughly. Set them aside for 5 minutes. Remove the chops from the marinade mixture and drain off the excess. Salt and pepper the chops generously. Preheat a dry cast-iron skillet for 3 minutes over high heat. Add the vegetable oil to the skillet and heat for 1 more minute. Place the chops in the hot oil and cook for 3 to 4 minutes per side for medium-rare or to desired degree of doneness.

Divide the Jicama and Red Cabbage Salad between two plates and top with the chops. Garnish with scallions and toasted sesame seeds. Serve at once.

Nutritional Analysis, includes jicama and red cabbage salad: 620 calories, FAT 47 g, PROTEIN 38 g, CARB 11 g, FIBER 3 g, CHOL 116 mg, IRON 3 mg, SODIUM 666 mg, CALC 97 mg

Jicama and Red Cabbage Salad

¼ teaspoon anise seeds

1 teaspoon vegetable oil

2 tablespoons freshly squeezed lime juice

¼ teaspoon Dijon mustard

Pinch of salt

½ cup julienned jicama (slices are ¹⁄₁₆ inch thick and may be cut with a mandoline)

½ cup shredded red cabbage

2 tablespoons coarsely chopped flat-leaf parsley

Heat the anise seeds in a small, dry skillet over high heat until fragrant. Transfer to a mortar and crush with a pestle or place in a Ziplock bag and crush with a mallet.

In a large bowl, stir together the vegetable oil, lime juice, crushed anise seeds, mustard, and salt. Toss in the jicama, red cabbage, and parsley and toss thoroughly.

Pan-Grilled Pork Chops with Mango–Black Pepper Glaze

You can make this glaze in the time it takes to pan grill the chops. It's that fast—and brightly flavored to boot.

MAKES 2 SERVINGS

Preparation time: 5 minutes

Cooking time: 15 to 20 minutes

½ cup white wine vinegar

1 teaspoon whole black peppercorns

¼ teaspoon sugar

½ medium mango, peeled and diced

Two 5- to 6-ounce pork loin chops

Salt and freshly milled black pepper to taste

Pour the vinegar into a small saucepan and bring to a boil over high heat. Add the peppercorns, sugar, and diced mango. Cook and reduce by a third, or until the liquid is a thick syrup, 4 to 5 minutes. Set aside.

Meanwhile, heat a cast-iron skillet over medium-high heat. Pat the chops dry with paper towels, then season to taste with salt and pepper. Pan grill about 5 minutes per side for medium.

Serve on warmed plates with a dollop of mango–black pepper glaze atop each.

Nutritional Analysis: 241 calories, FAT 7 g, PROTEIN 34 g, CARB 9 g, FIBER 1 g, CHOL 98 mg, IRON 2 mg, SODIUM 648 mg, CALC 34 mg

Menu Suggestion

To complete this meal and balance out the nutritional content, add a side of baby spinach, or mixed salad greens topped with your favorite vinaigrette. You'll be adding about 6 grams of carbohydrates and a goodly amount of that necessary fiber.

Health Benefit

Scientists have identified at least six compounds in black pepper that reduce the risk of hypertension.

Hazelnut-Crusted Pork Medallions on Red Beets

More commonly used in Europe than in the United States, hazelnuts make an aromatic crust and add an interesting flavor note to this pork dish.

Preparation time: 10 minutes
Cooking time: 20 minutes

MAKES 2 SERVINGS

10 ounces pork tenderloin, sliced into ½-inch thick rounds

1 teaspoon Dijon mustard

½ cup finely chopped hazelnuts

2 tablespoons chopped fresh basil

Salt and freshly milled black pepper to taste

2 tablespoons olive oil

1 cup low-sodium chicken broth

¼ cup half-and-half cream

1 cup sliced beets, drained

With a mallet or meat pounder, pound each pork round between sheets of wax paper until ¼ inch thickness. Mix the mustard, hazelnuts, basil, and salt and pepper in a bowl. Dredge the pork medallions in the mustard mixture and set it aside. Heat a dry skillet for 2 minutes, then add the oil and heat over medium-high heat for 1 minute. Add the dredged pork medallions and sauté for 30 seconds to 1 minute per side, until the nuts are lightly browned (the pork will finish cooking in the sauce). Remove the medallions from the pan and keep warm. Add the broth to the pan and deglaze, scraping up all of the brown bits that stick to the bottom. Stir in the cream and simmer for 3 more minutes. Return the medallions to the sauce and cook for 2 more minutes. Arrange the beet slices on two plates. Place each medallion over a beet slice and serve at once.

Nutritional Analysis: 565 calories, FAT 40 g, PROTEIN 37 g, CARB 15 g, FIBER 3 g, CHOL 109 mg, IRON 4 mg, SODIUM 230 mg, CALC 122 mg

Cooking Lesson

Interestingly, ½ cup of beets contains only 8 grams of carbohydrates, approximately the same number as an onion. While many people have unfavorable memories of beets from childhood (they are boring if served alone), their mouthwatering, sweet flavor can really enhance a dish. We think they make a colorful bed for many main courses, and have discovered that they are quite acceptable, as an accompaniment, straight from a can. Be careful not to buy sweetened pickled beets. They contain double the carbs.

You can roast fresh beets easily. Scrub beets, cut off the tops and wrap individually in aluminum foil. Roast in a 400°F oven 20 to 40 minutes, depending on their size. Remove foil, cool slightly, then peel the beets and serve. You'll love the taste: sweet, smoky, and mysterious.

Pan-Seared Pork Chops with Parma Relish

This relish is a perfect foil to the sweetness of the pork chop. It is also tasty served atop a grilled chicken breast or New York strip steak.

MAKES 2 SERVINGS

Preparation time: 15 minutes
Marinating time: 10 minutes
Cooking time: 6 minutes

RELISH

¼ cup chopped plum tomatoes

¼ cup chopped red onion

2 tablespoons red wine vinegar

2 tablespoons extra-virgin olive oil

1 garlic clove, chopped

2 tablespoons chopped fresh basil

1 teaspoon dried oregano

½ teaspoon salt

Freshly milled black pepper to taste

MARINADE

2 tablespoons red wine vinegar

2 tablespoons olive oil

1 garlic clove, chopped

Two 10-ounce thick-cut pork chops

Salt and freshly milled black pepper to taste

2 tablespoons vegetable oil

Chopped fresh flat-leaf parsley

Fresh Parmesan cheese curls for garnish

Toss the relish ingredients together in a small bowl. Set it aside.

Whisk marinade mixture in a shallow baking dish. Place the pork chops in the marinade, turning to coat both sides, and set aside for 10 minutes. Now remove the chops from the marinade and drain off the excess. Salt and pepper the chops generously. Preheat a dry cast-iron skillet for 3 minutes over high heat. Add the vegetable oil and heat for 1 more minute. Place the chops in the hot oil and cook to medium-rare, 3 to 4 minutes per side, or to desired degree of doneness.

Place the chops on a plate, top with relish, chopped parsley, and Parmesan cheese curls. Serve at once.

Nutritional Analysis: 580 calories, FAT 47 g, PROTEIN 32 g, CARB 8 g, FIBER 2 g, CHOL 90 mg, IRON 2 mg, SODIUM 1,224 mg, CALC 46 mg

Pork Tenders with Cumberland Sauce on a Bed of Spaghetti Squash

Autumn brings bracing weather, robust flavors, and colorful dinners. Cumberland sauce, a shiny-as-satin, sweet-sour, burgundy-colored, traditional English hunt sauce works well on chicken, pork, or game birds. You'll want to pair this sauce with a variety of meats.

Preparation time: 15 minutes
Cooking time: 15 minutes

MAKES 2 SERVINGS

1 teaspoon olive oil

12 ounces pork tenderloin, cut into 1-inch-thick medallions

½ teaspoon kosher salt

½ teaspoon freshly milled black pepper

1 tablespoon minced shallots

1 cup dry red wine

½ teaspoon cornstarch

Grated zest from ½ lemon plus 2 teaspoons fresh lemon juice

1 tablespoon all-fruit (no sugar added) red currant jelly

1 teaspoon Dijon mustard

2 cups Roasted Spaghetti Squash (page 48)

Heat a large skillet over medium-high heat, then film it with the oil. Meanwhile, dry the pork pieces on paper towels, and season with salt and pepper. Sauté until crisp and brown on the outside, and no longer pink in the middle, 3 to 4 minutes per side. Transfer to warmed dinner plates and reserve.

Add the shallots to the pan and cook about 30 seconds. Add the wine, bring to a boil, and reduce to about ¼ cup, 5 minutes or so. Dissolve the cornstarch in the lemon juice and whisk it into the sauce. Cook, stirring, until the sauce is thick and satiny-looking. Remove from the heat and stir in the jelly and mustard. Taste and adjust seasonings with salt and pepper.

To serve, make a nest of Roasted Spaghetti Squash on each plate and top with pork medallions and sauce.

Nutritional Analysis: 352 calories, FAT 12 g, PROTEIN 37 g, CARB 15 g, FIBER 3 g, CHOL 112 mg, IRON 3 mg, SODIUM 760 mg, CALC 56 mg

Pork Chops with Peach-Avocado Salsa on a Red Onion Confit

Modern American pork is as lean as a *Teen People* model. Want it to taste good? Cook it on a bed of flavorful red onion, then top it with spicy salsa. Yum. You'll never miss the fat, provided you don't overcook it. A quick pass through the oven is easy.

Preparation time: 15 minutes

Cooking time: 20 minutes

MAKES 2 SERVINGS

½ cup thinly sliced red onions

½ teaspoon dried oregano

1 teaspoon olive oil

Two 6-ounce center-cut pork chops

1 garlic clove, cut in half

½ teaspoon kosher salt, or to taste

½ teaspoon freshly milled black pepper, or to taste

SALSA

½ cup diced fresh or frozen peaches

½ cup diced ripe Hass avocado

1 tablespoon diced red onion

Grated zest and juice of 1 lime

⅛ teaspoon hot red pepper flakes, or to taste

1 teaspoon extra-virgin olive oil

Heat the oven to 450°F. Toss the onion slices with the oregano and olive oil. Preheat an oven-proof skillet on top of the stove over medium-high heat, then add the onion mixture. While the pan is heating, rub the chops on all sides with the garlic. Season the pork to taste with salt and pepper, and place on the onion mixture. Pop into the hot oven and cook until the pork is browned on the outside and no longer pink in the middle, about 15 minutes.

Meanwhile, stir together the salsa mixture in a small bowl. Cover and set it aside.

To serve, use a spatula to place half the onion and pork onto each of two dinner plates. Top with salsa.

Nutritional Analysis: 512 calories, FAT 6 g, PROTEIN 55 g, CARB 14 g, FIBER 4 g, CHOL 156 mg, IRON 3 mg, SODIUM 682 mg, CALC 58 mg

Cooking Lesson

Confit simply means "cooked in its own juices." The term originated in France, where frugal cooks preserved duck by cooking it in its own juices, then storing it in the fat in which it had cooked. We're talking months here, like all winter in a cave. (This was before electric refrigeration.) Today, a confit is a means of concentrating flavor, and to "confit" a vegetable or fruit concentrates the natural sugars and yields a delicious result.

Menu Suggestion

A big lettuce salad would look good on the plate and give you a little free crunch.

Roast Pork Loin with Apricots and Mustard on Red Cabbage

Each slice of pork loin you fan out over the red cabbage will have an orange-colored core, a burst of apricot color, and flavor. Remember that you needn't cook pork to death, either. An internal temperature of 160°F is all that's required.

MAKES 2 SERVINGS

Preparation time: 10 minutes

Cooking time: 20 to 25 minutes

12 ounces pork loin

3 dried apricots, coarsely chopped (about 2 tablespoons)

2 garlic cloves, minced

2 tablespoons minced fresh flat-leaf Italian parsley

1 teaspoon olive oil, plus extra for filming the pan

½ teaspoon kosher salt

½ teaspoon freshly milled black pepper

2 tablespoons Dijon mustard

2 cups finely shredded red cabbage

1 teaspoon rice wine vinegar

Heat the oven to 425°F. Use a sharpening steel, boning knife, or a sturdy chopstick to poke a hole lengthwise through the center of the meat and insert the apricots into this hole, pushing them with your fingers.

Combine the garlic and parsley with the olive oil on a sheet of wax paper. Season the roast all over with salt and pepper, then slather it with mustard. Dredge the roast in the garlic and parsley mixture. Toss the shredded cabbage with the vinegar in a medium bowl, and season to taste with salt and pepper.

Film the roasting pan with olive oil and make a bed of the red cabbage on the bottom of the pan. Place the pork on the cabbage and roast, uncovered, for 20 to 25 minutes, or until the internal temperature of the meat is 160°F. Let it stand 5 to 10 minutes, then carve into ½-inch slices and serve, making a bed of braised cabbage topped with fanned-out slices of meat on each plate.

Nutritional Analysis: 427 calories, FAT 25 g, PROTEIN 36 g, CARB 13 g, FIBER 3 g, CHOL 107 mg, IRON 3 mg, SODIUM 975 mg, CALC 103 mg

Health Benefit

Once again, cabbage gives a dish not only a flavor lift, but a nutritional boost as well. You'll get 59 percent of your RDA for vitamin C, and from the meat, 33 percent of the iron you require.

Caramelized Pork with Scallions and Butter Lettuce

Vietnamese cooking combines the best of Asia and Europe. Discovering that it is light on carbs is almost too good to be true.

MAKES 2 SERVINGS

Preparation time: 15 minutes

Cooking time: 20 minutes

1 tablespoon peanut oil

12 ounces pork tenderloin, cut into bite-size cubes

1 teaspoon brown sugar

1 tablespoon water

1 tablespoon fish sauce (nuoc mam)

½ cup low-sodium chicken broth

¼ teaspoon white pepper

½ teaspoon ground cinnamon

1 cup diagonally cut, 2-inch pieces of scallions

1 head butter lettuce, torn into bite-size pieces

2 tablespoons rice vinegar

¼ cup fresh basil leaves, cut into chiffonade (see note)

¼ cup chopped fresh cilantro

Heat a large skillet over medium-high heat, then film it with the oil. Add the pork and cook until brown on all sides, about 5 minutes. Meanwhile, in a small saucepan, cook the sugar and water together over medium-high heat until the sugar caramelizes, about 5 minutes. Stir in the fish sauce, chicken broth, white pepper, and cinnamon. Pour over pork and toss to mix. Add the scallions. Cover and steam 3 to 5 minutes.

Toss lettuce with rice vinegar, basil, and cilantro in a mixing bowl. Add the cooked pork mixture. Divide between two plates and serve at once.

Nutritional Analysis: 349 calories, FAT 17 g, PROTEIN 38 g, CARB 8 g, FIBER 3 g, CHOL 118 mg, IRON 3 mg, SODIUM 1,027 mg, CALC 53 mg

Cooking Lesson

Cutting herbs or leafy green vegetables into chiffonade yields great flavor and is really easy to do. Make a stack of leaves, then roll them up like a cigar. Using a sharp chef's knife with the point held against the cutting board, cut fine slices, and you'll have gorgeous chiffonade. No bruising of the herb, just opening it up for maximum flavor.

Sesame-Glazed Pork Chops on a Bed of Cauliflower

Look to the Far East for great flavor profiles. Buy small jars of sesame seeds and sesame oil and keep them in the refrigerator or freezer to prevent them from going rancid. Always taste first if you've had them awhile. The sharp, bitter taste of old oils is unmistakable.

MAKES 2 SERVINGS

Preparation time: 10 minutes

Cooking time: 15 minutes

Two 6-ounce center-cut pork chops, about 1-inch thick

½ teaspoon kosher salt

½ teaspoon freshly milled black pepper

1 teaspoon dark sesame oil

1 teaspoon toasted sesame seeds

¼ cup low-sodium chicken broth

½ teaspoon sugar

1 tablespoon red wine vinegar

1 teaspoon Dijon mustard

3 cups cauliflorets

Heat a large skillet over medium-high heat. Season the pork chops with salt and pepper. Film the pan with the sesame oil. Brown the chops on both sides, about 3 minutes per side. Sprinkle the chops with the sesame seeds and cook 1 more minute. Add chicken broth, sugar, vinegar, and mustard and whisk together in the pan. Cover the pan, reduce the heat, and cook about 20 minutes, or until the chops are tender.

Meanwhile, steam the cauliflower in the microwave with a couple of tablespoons of water on high (100 percent power) until tender, about 7 minutes. Alternatively, boil in a saucepan of water for 10 minutes. Drain.

To serve, make a bed of cauliflower, then top with chops. Spoon the sauce over all.

Nutritional Analysis: 353 calories, FAT 14 g, PROTEIN 48 g, CARB 10 g, FIBER 4 g, CHOL 131 mg, IRON 3 mg. SODIUM 894 mg, CALC 79 mg

Cooking Lesson

Browning meat in a pan and then completing the cooking in a liquid is known as braising. It is not necessary or desirable to overcook the pork. Brown it well, then add the sauce ingredients, cover, and cook until just barely tender. The meat should still be slightly pink at the center.

Bitter Greens with Prosciutto, Feta, and Dried Apricots

Taking the bitter with the sweet has long been one surefire trail to tabletop nirvana. Toss bitter greens with vinaigrette, then top with salty sweet prosciutto, feta, and sweet apricots. A pot of tea, a friend—it's lunch.

Preparation time: 10 minutes

MAKES 2 SERVINGS

4 cups mixed bitter greens (such as escarole, endive, beet greens, radicchio)

¼ cup chopped fresh flat-leaf parsley leaves

3 ounces thinly sliced prosciutto cut into bite-size pieces

2 ounces feta cheese, cubed

2 tablespoons dried apricots, coarsely chopped

4 large hard-cooked eggs

DRESSING

½ teaspoon kosher salt

1 tablespoon balsamic vinegar

1 teaspoon Dijon mustard

3 tablespoons extra-virgin olive oil

Freshly milled black pepper

Toss the greens, parsley, prosciutto, feta, and apricots in a large salad bowl. Whisk together the dressing ingredients in a small bowl and drizzle over the salad. Toss to mix and divide between two chilled dinner plates. Top with hard-cooked eggs, cut in half.

Nutritional Analysis: 508 calories, FAT 39 g, PROTEIN 27 g, CARB 15 g, FIBER 4 g, CHOL 478 mg, IRON 5 mg, SODIUM 1,531 mg, CALC 258 mg

Cooking Lesson

If you want more greens with this lunch, feel free. After all . . . most crisp green lettuces are free. So go ahead, turn yourself into a rabbit, but be sure to keep the protein load up. When we first started making this salad, it was a little skimpy in the protein department before we remembered the ubiquitous egg. It both tasted great and balanced the nutritional load.

CHICKEN: ONE FOR EVERY POT

The subtle flavor of chicken offers a wonderful

opportunity to explore unlimited flavoring options. You can show off the delicious taste of a single seasoning, such as thyme (our herb of choice if we could only pick one with which to be stranded on a deserted island), or use it as a neutral background for a complex sauce with a combination of exotic flavors. Chicken can be dreadfully bland and dry when improperly handled, or it can be a cold knockout.

Food safety is no joke with chicken. It is only safe when it is cooked to 160°F. Besides, in our opinion, the flavor really improves with cooking. The easiest way to check for doneness is with an instant-read thermometer. At the thickest part of the chicken piece or the breast of the whole bird, the thermometer should read 160 to 165°F. You can also check by making a cut in the meat. You should see no red or pink color whatsoever. Buy an instant meat thermometer. It's a great $10 investment that will make you feel like a four-star restaurant chef.

Equally important is how you handle raw chicken. Most salmonella cases are a result of using a knife or cutting board to cut up a tomato for the salad after it was used to cut raw chicken. Wash all forks, knives, and cutting boards with hot soapy water after they've come in contact with raw chicken pieces and have no fear. Salmonella is not a very hearty pathogen and with careful washing, there is really no chance of cross contamination.

We recommend buying premium-grade chickens, such as Bell and Evans, D'Artagnan, or Murray's. Or you may have a local favorite. We also like Empire kosher chickens. The salting process involved in preparing kosher meat improves the taste and texture of chicken.

Another great quality about chicken is that it freezes really well, making it easy to keep on hand for emergency dinners. Buy it when you see it on sale and double wrap it. It keeps in the freezer for up to two months. After that, it is still good for chicken soup.

In this chapter we have come up with some fast recipes that may surprise you. We like breasts and thighs alike. If you have gotten accustomed to eating just breasts, we encourage you to be venturesome and try thighs. With the skin removed there is very little fat difference, and the dark meat tastes richer, more chicken-y to us.

Chicken with Leeks and Tomatoes

Add a tossed salad, a glass of red wine and before you know it, dinner's on.

MAKES 2 SERVINGS

Preparation time: 15 minutes

Cooking time: 20 minutes

2 slices thick-cut peppered bacon

2 boneless, skinless chicken breasts
  (10 ounces total), split and pounded
  to ¼-inch thickness

1 tablespoon unsalted butter

1 medium leek, cut in half lengthwise,
  washed, then sliced crosswise using
  2 inches of the green part plus the bulb

½ cup half-and-half

1 tablespoon chopped fresh tarragon, or
  1 teaspoon dried

½ teaspoon hot red pepper flakes

3 plum tomatoes, chopped

½ teaspoon kosher salt

½ teaspoon freshly milled black pepper

Cook the bacon until crisp in a 10-inch skillet, then drain on a paper towel. Cook the chicken breasts in the rendered bacon fat over medium-high heat until golden brown and fork-tender, about 10 minutes. Remove the chicken from the skillet and reserve.

Add the butter to the skillet, then cook the sliced leeks until crisp-tender, about 10 minutes. Stir in the half-and-half, tarragon, and hot pepper flakes and boil until slightly thickened. Crumble the bacon into the sauce, then stir in the tomatoes. Return the chicken to the pan with any juices that have accumulated on the plate. Heat a couple of minutes, then season with salt and pepper and divide between two warmed dinner plates.

Nutritional Analysis: 447 calories, FAT 27 g, PROTEIN 38 g, CARB 9 g, FIBER 2 g, CHOL 143 mg, IRON 2 mg, SODIUM 892 mg, CALC 100 mg

Cooking Lesson

Combining bacon fat with butter will create a subtle, satisfying taste you've had before—in fine restaurants, where chefs often employ this technique. It lifts the humble chicken breast to new heights.

Stir-Fried Chicken on Bitter Greens

Think of this as a Thai-style entrée. Finish your meal with fresh melon or berries.

MAKES 2 SERVINGS

Preparation time: 15 minutes
Cooking time: 15 minutes

4 cups bitter salad greens (any mixture of watercress, arugula, Belgian endive, bok choy, spinach), rinsed and spun dry

1 tablespoon rice vinegar

SAUCE

1 garlic clove, pressed

¼ teaspoon sugar

2 tablespoons dry sherry

2 tablespoons Thai fish sauce (nom pla)

½ teaspoon grated fresh ginger

2 boneless, skinless chicken breasts (10 ounces total), split and pounded to ¼-inch thickness

1 tablespoon peanut oil

½ onion, quartered and separated into single layers

Compose the greens on two dinner plates and drizzle with vinegar, then set them aside. Whisk together the ingredients for the sauce in a small bowl.

Cut the pounded chicken across the grain into 1-inch-wide strips.

Heat a skillet or wok over high heat, then add the oil and the onion. Stir-fry until the onion edges begin to brown. Scoop the onion into a bowl and reserve.

Add the chicken and stir-fry until it begins to brown on the edges and is thoroughly opaque and cooked through, about 2 minutes. Scoop the chicken into the bowl with the onions.

Add the sauce mixture to the wok and stir to free any browned bits. Return the chicken and onions to the pan and stir until the sauce cooks down, about 3 minutes more. Spoon over greens and serve immediately.

Nutritional Analysis: 395 calories; FAT 18 g, PROTEIN 47 g, CARB 7 g, FIBER 1 g, CHOL 130 mg, IRON 2 mg, SODIUM 1,464 mg, CALC 67 mg

Cooking Lesson

Use the Asian technique of cooking everything in the same pan—just not at once—and you'll get that crisp-tender, flavorful result you love when you eat out. It takes practice and a lot of attention. Do all your cutting ahead, get the necessary bowls and props around you (*mise en place,* as they say in culinary school). You'll soon love this technique.

Garlic Lime Chicken

Infusing chicken breast with the flavor of garlic and lime creates a puckery, smoky, mouthwatering effect. When cooked on an outdoor or indoor grill, the charred grill marks, which are the caramelized sugars in the meat, add an excellent contrast to the sour lime. Serve atop one of our vegetable purées.

Preparation time: 5 minutes
Marinating time: 20 minutes
Cooking time: 10 minutes

MAKES 2 SERVINGS

2 tablespoons low sodium soy sauce
Grated zest and juice of 1 lime
1 teaspoon Worcestershire sauce
1 garlic clove, minced
½ teaspoon dry mustard

2 boneless, skinless chicken breasts
 (10 ounces total), split and pounded
 to ¼-inch thickness
½ teaspoon cracked black pepper

Combine the soy sauce, lime juice and zest, Worcestershire sauce, garlic, and mustard in a glass dish or resealable plastic bag. Add the chicken and turn to coat with the mixture. Cover the chicken and refrigerate for 20 minutes.

Remove the chicken from the marinade and pepper it thoroughly. Discard the marinade.

Preheat a grill or skillet over medium-high heat. Film it with olive oil. Cook the chicken until golden on both sides and opaque and cooked through, about 10 minutes in total.

Serve hot or at room temperature garnished with additional lime zest.

Nutritional Analysis: 302 calories, FAT 11 g, PROTEIN 44 g, CARB 3 g, FIBER .25 g, CHOL 119 mg, IRON 2 mg, SODIUM 656 mg, CALC 33 mg

Cooking Lesson
Sometimes half the battle is won by patience. Just let the chicken swim along in this aromatic marinade, and the flavor will be so much better.

Menu Suggestion
You can afford a sweet temptation with this meal. Buy or make sugar-free meringue shells (page 174) and serve alongside ½ cup of berries. You'll only have added 3.5 grams of carbohydrates with the meringues and 5 grams or so with ½ cup of raspberries or strawberries.

Szechuan Peanut Chicken

Despite the convention that says you have to serve this chicken atop rice, we find it's terrific served in a rimmed soup bowl as a one-dish dinner.

Preparation time: 15 minutes
Cooking time: 15 minutes

MAKES 2 SERVINGS

2 boneless, skinless chicken breasts
   (10 ounces total), split and pounded
   to ¼-inch thickness
1 tablespoon low sodium soy sauce
1 tablespoon cornstarch

SEASONING SAUCE
2 tablespoons low sodium soy sauce
1 tablespoon dry sherry
1 tablespoon rice wine vinegar

1 teaspoon sugar
1 teaspoon sesame oil

1 tablespoon peanut oil
4 medium dried red cayenne peppers
½ green bell pepper, julienned
1 stalk celery, thinly sliced on the diagonal
¼ cup roasted peanuts
1 scallion, green and white parts, chopped

Cut the chicken into bite-size pieces and place in a glass bowl. In a small bowl, mix the soy sauce and cornstarch into a smooth paste and combine with the chicken. Stir to coat all the pieces, then cover and set aside for 10 minutes.

Whisk all the ingredients for the seasoning sauce in a small bowl and set aside.

Preheat a wok or large skillet, then add the oil. Stir-fry the dried red peppers until blackened, about 1 minute. Add the chicken pieces and stir-fry until the chicken begins to brown, about 2 minutes. Add the green pepper and celery and stir-fry until crunchy, no more than 2 minutes.

Add the seasoning sauce and stir until thickened and hot—just 1 minute or so. Remove from the heat and stir in the peanuts and scallions. Mix together then divide between two rimmed soup bowls.

Nutritional Analysis: 439 calories, FAT 22 g, PROTEIN 46 g, CARB 13 g, FIBER 2 g, CHOL 119 mg, IRON 2 mg, SODIUM 951 mg, CAL 48 mg

Cooking Lesson

You'll notice there is a spoonful of sugar in the sauce. Sometimes, nothing else will do. And the damage to the total number of carbohydrate grams in the dish is minimal, nothing like the real thing.

Gin-and-Orange-Juice–Soaked Chicken with Onions

Hard day at the office? Start the chicken marinating, then drink a shot of that gin yourself. Sometimes it's worth it.

MAKES 2 SERVINGS

Marinating time: 10 minutes

Cooking time: 15 to 20 minutes

2 teaspoons fresh or frozen orange juice

2 tablespoons gin

½ teaspoon dried oregano

½ teaspoon hot red pepper flakes

½ teaspoon kosher salt

2 tablespoons peanut oil

2 boneless, skinless chicken breasts (10 ounces total), split and pounded to ¼-inch thickness

1 medium onion, thinly sliced

In a bowl or resealable plastic bag, combine the orange juice, gin, oregano, red pepper, salt, and 1 tablespoon oil. Add the chicken breasts and onions and set the mixture aside to marinate, covered or sealed, about 10 minutes.

Heat a large skillet over medium-high heat for 1 minute. Add the remaining tablespoon of peanut oil. Lift the chicken from the marinade and pat dry, reserving the marinade and onions. Place the breasts in the hot skillet, smooth side down. Cook about 7 minutes, then turn and cook for 3 more minutes on the second side. Add the reserved marinade and onions to the pan. The gin and orange juice mixture will steam through the seared meat. Cook, turning the chicken once or twice more, until the onions are brown, heaping them atop the chicken as they begin to color. By this point the chicken will be cooked through and the sauce nearly evaporated. (Cut into the thickest part of the chicken to check: it should be opaque white.) Divide between two dinner plates and serve.

Nutritional Analysis: 461 calories, FAT 25 g, PROTEIN 43 g, CARB 7 g, FIBER 1 g, CHOL 119 mg, IRON 2 mg, SODIUM 684 mg, CALC 39 mg

Cooking Lesson

Boneless, skinless chicken breast is the most popular yet perhaps the least flavorful cut of chicken. Marinating it in a mixture of spirits and acid makes it more palatable. If you're out of gin, try vodka or tequila, and squeeze in a lemon. You won't change the nutritional analysis appreciably, and you'll still have a pumped up flavor to your chicken breast that's golden on the outside, succulent in the middle.

Menu Suggestion

Add a huge spinach salad to complete this dinner. Mix celery, scallions, and an avocado in with the spinach. Crumble goat cheese (we love Laura Chenel's new Norse cheese) on top, and dress with your favorite vinaigrette. This will add about 9 grams of carbohydrates and 12 grams of protein per serving.

Shirley's Sautéed Sherry Chicken

Keep packages of chicken tenders or boneless, skinless chicken breasts handy for quick, brightly flavored dinners you can have on the table in a flash.

MAKES 2 SERVINGS

Preparation time: 15 minutes

Cooking time: 15 minutes (concurrent)

2 boneless, skinless chicken breasts
(10 ounces total), split and pounded
to ¼-inch thickness
½ teaspoon kosher salt
½ teaspoon freshly milled black pepper
1 teaspoon olive oil
1 teaspoon unsalted butter

½ cup finely chopped onion
2 garlic cloves, chopped
1 teaspoon Dijon mustard
2 teaspoons sherry vinegar
1 tablespoon extra-virgin olive oil
4 cups mesclun or mixed baby lettuces
1 teaspoon dried cranberries

Season the chicken with salt and pepper. Heat a skillet over medium-high heat, then add the olive oil and butter. Cook the chopped onion and garlic until transluscent, about 4 minutes. Move the vegetables to the sides of the pan to make room for the chicken. Place the breasts in the pan and let them cook undisturbed until they begin to brown on the edges, about 2 minutes. Turn once and continue to cook until the chicken is done, about 2 more minutes.

Stir together the mustard and vinegar in a small bowl. Spoon ½ teaspoon of the mixture into a mixing bowl and set aside. Pour the rest over the chicken and onion mixture in the pan. Cook and stir 1 more minute.

While the chicken is cooking, whisk the extra-virgin olive oil into the mustard mixture in the mixing bowl. Toss the salad greens in this vinaigrette, then divide between two plates. Top with cooked chicken and finish with dried cranberries. Serve at once.

Nutritional Analysis: 436 calories, FAT 23 g, PROTEIN 45 g, CARB 12 g, FIBER 3 g,
CHOL 124 mg, IRON 3 mg, SODIUM 774 mg, CALC 120 mg

Cooking Lesson

In this recipe we simply transfer a part of the mustard-vinegar mixture
we're using to sauce the chicken in the salad bowl, add oil, and whisk.
Never let raw meat touch or contaminate any dressing that is not to be
cooked. This is the most common way salmonella is transferred in
kitchens.

Mustard both thickens and flavors whatever dish we use it in. Here it
makes a fine binder for the chicken as well as the salad. Always use
the best quality mustard you can lay your hands on.

Menu Suggestion

Add a ½-cup serving of steamed cauliflower to this basic menu, and
you have increased the fiber content by almost half, while only raising
the calories by 25 and the carbohydrates by 2 or 3 grams.

East Indian Chicken with Spinach and Farmers' Cheese

Saag paneer, the Indian spinach dish studded with fresh cheese, makes a soothing counterpoint to a hot and spicy sautéed chicken in coconut gravy. These big flavors satisfy your appetite without breaking the carbohydrate bank.

MAKES 2 SERVINGS

Preparation time: 15 minutes

Cooking time: 15 minutes (concurrent)

DRY RUB

½ teaspoon cayenne, or to taste

1 teaspoon garam masala, or 1 teaspoon
   curry powder with ½ teaspoon hot paprika

½ teaspoon ground turmeric

½ teaspoon kosher salt

½ teaspoon white pepper

2 boneless, skinless chicken thighs
   (10 ounces total)

2 teaspoons peanut oil

¼ cup sliced onion

2 garlic cloves, smashed

¼ cup coarsely chopped tomato

1 pound baby spinach leaves, very well
   washed

2 tablespoons grated fresh ginger

½ cup unsweetened coconut milk

Salt and pepper to taste

2 ounces fresh cheese squares (farmer's
   cheese, string cheese, or *Cuajada an
   Terron*)

Black sesame seeds for garnish

Stir together the dry rub ingredients in a small bowl. Cut the chicken thighs into 1-inch-wide strips. Coat them with the dry rub, reserving any remaining mixture.

Heat a large skillet over very high heat. Add the oil and preheat. Cook the chicken strips, turning them with tongs, until cooked through and golden on the outside, about 5 minutes. Transfer to a warm plate.

Add the onion slices to the hot pan and cook until they begin to brown, about 6 minutes. Add the garlic and cook a few minutes more. Add the tomato and cook, stirring a moment longer. Add the spinach in handfuls, stirring until it begins to wilt before adding another batch. Once all the spinach is in the skillet, sprinkle it with the reserved dry rub, stir, then cover and cook 2 to 3 minutes longer.

Stir in the grated ginger and half of the coconut milk. Taste and adjust the seasonings with salt and pepper. Transfer to a food processor or blender and puree until smooth. Remove the blade and stir in the cheese squares, cover, and set the mixture aside.

Meanwhile, add the remaining coconut milk to the hot pan and boil over medium-high heat until reduced by one-third, about 5 minutes. Return the chicken pieces to the pan. Taste and adjust seasonings with salt and pepper.

To serve, divide the spinach mixture between two warmed dinner plates. Place chicken and gravy alongside. Sprinkle the plate with black sesame seeds.

Nutritional Analysis: 519 calories, FAT 29 g, PROTEIN 51 g, CARB 15 g, FIBER 8 g, CHOL 169 mg, IRON 9 mg, SODIUM 1,099 mg, CALC 462 mg

Cooking Lesson

This dish yields 115 percent of the vitamin A, 46 percent of the vitamin C, 28 percent of the iron, and 23 percent of the calcium needed daily for a healthy diet. You can make it ahead, store covered in the refrigerator, then reheat it in the microwave a few moments.

Menu Suggestion

Serve a cooling raita alongside this dish. That's simply slivers of cucumber in plain yogurt. A pot of tea, some fresh honeydew melon for dessert. Including the raita, total calories: 382.5. Total carbs: 15 grams.

Quatres Épices–Grilled Chicken on Cabbage and Red Pepper Salad

If you have ever wondered how to make a chicken breast stand up and whistle Dixie, this is it. Bright flavors, bold colors, and lots of crunch make this a dinner you'll want twice a week. That's a good idea, because the salad makes enough to feed four—it keeps well in the refrigerator and makes a great "free lunch" the next day. You can double the spice blend and cook four pieces of meat at one time, saving two for lunch. Shred all the salad ingredients in the food processor using the slicing blade, and you'll have the work done in no time.

Preparation time: 20 minutes
Chilling time: 30 minutes (concurrent)
Cooking time: 10 minutes

MAKES 2 SERVINGS

4 cups finely shredded green cabbage
3 tablespoons red wine vinegar
½ cup thinly sliced red bell pepper

DRESSING
One 1.7-ounce can flat anchovy fillets, drained
6 garlic cloves, minced
3 tablespoons minced fresh flat-leaf parsley
2 tablespoons extra-virgin olive oil

2 boneless, skinless chicken breasts
   (10 ounces total), split and pounded
   to ¼-inch thickness
1 teaspoon extra-virgin olive oil
1 tablespoon *quatres épices* seasoning (see
   note)
Freshly milled black pepper
Kosher salt to taste

Sprinkle the cabbage with vinegar, then toss in a large bowl. Arrange the pepper on top of the cabbage, cover, and refrigerate until serving time. To make the dressing, crush and blend the ingredients with a mortar and pestle (or use a food processor with the steel blade). Set it aside.

Dab the chicken breasts with the olive oil, then rub in the *quatres épices,* salt and pepper. Heat a ridged grill pan or a sauté pan over high heat. Cook the meat on one side without disturbing, until brown on the edges, about 3 minutes. Turn and cook the second side until the chicken is cooked through, 5 to 8 minutes total.

Mound one-quarter of the cabbage mixture on a dinner plate and top with a grilled chicken breast. Just before serving, toss the cabbage and pepper with the dressing.

NOTE: Buy commercially prepared *quatres épices*, or blend your own by grinding together ¼ teaspoon each cinnamon, cloves, allspice, and nutmeg. You may use a mortar and pestle or a spice grinder.

Nutritional Analysis: 401 calories, FAT 25 g, PROTEIN 33 g, CARB 14g, FIBER 5 g,
CHOL 80 mg, IRON 4 mg, SODIUM 1,548 mg, CALC 165 mg

Cooking Lesson

You'll get 126 percent of the vitamin C and 46 percent of the iron you need for a healthy diet from this colorful, one-dish dinner. To lower the sodium, reduce the amount of anchovies in the salad dressing.

Menu Suggestion

Don't forget about those sugar-free Popsicles and ice cream bars. They'll add virtually no carbohydrates to your dinner and will provide a sweet finish.

Grilled Lemon Chicken with Gremolata

Whose freezer doesn't contain the ubiquitous chicken breasts? And who hasn't gotten sick and tired of eating them? One trick is to marinate them for a few minutes in plain old lemon juice, then sear them on the outside to create a golden glaze. Don't overcook them, and top them with a shot of this ancient Italian secret, gremolata. Nothing more than an ad-lib mixture of finely minced lemon (or orange) zest, parsley, and garlic; it will make that chicken fly.

Should you have some chicken left over, make an impromptu niçoise-style salad the next day, tossing cooked chicken with niçoise olives, hard-cooked eggs, lettuce, and wedges of terrific tomatoes. Finish with drops of extra-virgin olive oil and lemon juice.

MAKES 2 SERVINGS

Preparation time: 10 minutes
Marinating time: 15 minutes maximum
Cooking time: 5 minutes

2 boneless, skinless chicken breasts (10 ounces total), split and pounded to ¼-inch thickness
Juice of 1 lemon
1 teaspoon extra-virgin olive oil
Kosher salt and freshly milled black pepper to taste

GREMOLATA
2 tablespoons minced garlic cloves
2 tablespoons minced fresh flat-leaf parsley
2 tablespoons minced lemon zest

Dry the chicken on paper towels. Place in a bowl and sprinkle with lemon juice. Dab with oil, and season with salt and pepper. Set aside for up to 15 minutes. Stir the ingredients for the gremolata, and set aside.

Preheat a ridged grill pan until smoking hot. Add the chicken, cooking just until golden grill marks begin to show, no more than 2 to 3 minutes. Turn and finish cooking on the second side, about 4 minutes total.

To serve, place a chicken breast on a warmed dinner plate and top with a shot of gremolata.

Nutritional Analysis: 320 calories, FAT 13 g, PROTEIN 43 g, CARB 5, FIBER 1 g, CHOL 119 mg, IRON 2 mg, SODIUM 685 mg, CALC 48 mg

Cooking Lesson

Hidden assets in this recipe come by way of the gremolata. You'll get nearly 40 percent of your daily requirement for vitamin C and 27 percent for iron just by munching on the lemon and parsley. Not to mention the health benefits from garlic. First, there's the vampire factor. Eat this much garlic, and you're safe from any Dracula. Second, your heart will pound all the more securely from the micronutrients found in garlic.

Menu Suggestion

Make an ad-lib salad using as much arugula as you'd like, tossed with clementine or tangerine wedges and your own vinaigrette (see the choices in the Extras chapter). You'll only add 5 to 10 carbohydrate grams if you serve 1 piece of fruit for two people, and you will have upped that vitamin C even more.

Chicken Jamaica

From a hot and balmy Island comes this quick skillet stew. Serve it alongside spaghetti squash for a colorful, crunchy, hot-and-sweet supper.

Preparation time: 15 minutes

Cooking time: 25 minutes (concurrent)

MAKES 2 SERVINGS

2 teaspoons extra-virgin olive oil

½ cup chopped onion

3 garlic cloves, finely chopped

2 boneless, skinless chicken thighs (10 ounces total)

½ teaspoon curry powder

½ teaspoon freshly milled black pepper

½ teaspoon kosher salt

½ teaspoon ground allspice

½ teaspoon hot red pepper flakes

1 cup chopped tomato

2 tablespoons drained capers

¼ cup dry red wine

1 bay leaf

1 teaspoon dried thyme

1 teaspoon chopped fresh chives

Heat a large skillet over medium heat. Add the oil and onion. Cook and stir until it begins to turn golden, about 3 minutes, then add the garlic. While they are cooking, place the chicken thighs on a piece of wax paper. In a small bowl, mix the curry, pepper, salt, allspice, and red pepper flakes. Rub the spice mixture into the chicken pieces, then brown them in the skillet, pushing the onions to the sides. After you have turned the chicken once, add the tomato and capers. Cook 2 to 3 minutes, then add the wine, bay leaf, and thyme. Cover and cook until chicken is tender, about 20 minutes.

Serve sprinkled with chives.

Nutritional Analysis: 420 calories, FAT 21 g, PROTEIN 40 g, CARB 14 g, FIBER 3 g, CHOL 135 mg, IRON 3 mg, SODIUM 623 mg, CALC 89 mg

Cooking Lesson

If you wish to guarantee that chicken will cook evenly, pound each chicken piece between sheets of wax paper, using the bottom of a glass or a mallet, until it is even. It need not necessarily be thin, simply of a uniform thickness.

Smoky Mustard Greens Soup

Soups not only provide satisfying meals, they also convey tremendous health benefits when laced with greens. Use flavorful low-fat turkey sausages, and you slash the fat grams as well as the carbs. Got a big family? Double or quadruple this recipe measure for measure and feed the multitudes. All you need is a bigger pot.

Preparation time: 15 minutes
Cooking time: 15 minutes

MAKES 2 SERVINGS

8 ounces low-fat Italian sweet chicken or
    turkey sausage, cut into bite-sized pieces
2 slices bacon, chopped
¼ cup chopped onion
1 garlic clove, smashed
1 cup canned tomatoes with their juices,
    chopped

2 cups low-sodium chicken broth
½ teaspoon kosher salt
½ teaspoon freshly milled black pepper
4 cups fresh mustard greens, washed, center
    ribs removed, greens chopped

Heat a large soup pot over medium-high heat. Add the sausage and bacon and cook, stirring, until they brown, about 10 minutes. Add the onion and garlic about halfway through and cook and stir until the onion begins to brown. Stir in the tomatoes, broth, and salt and pepper and cook about 10 minutes. Add the mustard greens and simmer the soup just long enough to wilt the greens, no more than 3 to 5 minutes; they should still be bright green and tender. Serve immediately.

Nutritional Analysis: 234 calories, FAT 15 g, PROTEIN 20 g, CARB 7 g, FIBER 3 g,
CHOL 56 mg, IRON 2 mg, SODIUM 988 mg, CALC 100 mg

Health Benefit

Eat yourself silly with this soup. You'll be getting 124 percent of the RDA for vitamin A as well as 157 percent for vitamin C, not to mention 26 percent for iron. It's all those greens combined with tomatoes and onion.

Sweet Chicken Sausage Tagine

The Moroccan tagine, rich and colorful, is named for the pot in which its cooked. You can successfully duplicate this dish by cooking it in a porcelain-clad cast-iron baker (such as Le Creuset) or another large heavy stewpan. The blend of fresh vegetables with crunchy almonds, sweet raisins, and sausage makes for a satisfying dinner. Prep the vegetables while you brown the sausages. For those who aren't counting carbs, serve this stew over a bed of couscous. Half a cup of couscous yields 100 calories and 20 carbohydrate grams.

MAKES 2 SERVINGS

Preparation time: 20 minutes
Cooking time: 30 minutes

8 ounces low-fat Italian sweet chicken or turkey sausage, cut into bite-size pieces

2 teaspoons olive oil

¼ cup chopped onion

2 garlic cloves, chopped

¼ cup chopped canned tomatoes with their juices

2 cups (15½-ounce can) low-sodium chicken broth

1 tablespoon slivered almonds

1 teaspoon raisins

1 teaspoon ground ginger

1 teaspoon sweet paprika

½ teaspoon ground cinnamon

⅛ teaspoon saffron threads

¼ cup fresh or frozen green beans cut into 2-inch lengths

¼ cup 1-inch pieces of red bell pepper

1 tablespoon fresh lemon juice

1 teaspoon harissa, hot sauce, or Chinese chili paste to taste (see note)

½ teaspoon kosher salt

½ teaspoon freshly milled black pepper

Place the sausage in a skillet and cook over medium-high heat, adding the oil as needed to prevent sticking. Turn frequently until browned on all sides.

Stir in the onion and garlic and cook until golden, 3 to 5 minutes. Add the tomatoes, chicken broth, almonds, raisins, ginger, paprika, cinnamon, and saffron and bring to a boil. Add the beans. Simmer for about 10 minutes, then add the peppers and cook an additional 5 to 7 minutes. Just before serving, stir in the lemon juice and harissa, and season with salt and pepper.

NOTE: Harissa is a North African (Tunisian) condiment you can buy in specialty markets. Not only does this condiment zip up soup, it also makes fried eggs sing a desert lament.

Nutritional Analysis: 330 calories, FAT 22 g, PROTEIN 22 g, CARB 14 g, FIBER 3 g, CHOL 90 mg, IRON 4 mg, SODIUM 2,350 mg, CALC 70 mg

Ball Park Mustard Chicken on a Bed of Baby Spinach

A jar of hot and spicy ball park mustard is a good thing to keep on hand. Slather mustard over chicken breasts, and even the lamest-tasting chicken develops character.

Preparation time: 10 minutes

Cooking time: 15 minutes

MAKES 2 SERVINGS

¼ cup plain yogurt

1 tablespoon ball park (or other spicy) mustard

¼ teaspoon kosher salt

¼ teaspoon cayenne

2 boneless, skinless chicken breasts (10 ounces total), split and pounded to ¼-inch thickness

One 12-ounce package baby spinach

1 teaspoon olive oil

Preheat the oven to 400°F. Stir the yogurt, mustard, salt, and cayenne in a bowl. Rub the chicken breast cutlets with the yogurt mixture and place on a greased baking sheet. Roast about 20 minutes, or until cooked through.

Meanwhile, wash the spinach leaves but do not dry. Heat a large skillet, then film it with oil. Add the spinach by the handful. Cook and stir until the spinach is limp. Transfer to two warmed dinner plates. Top with chicken breasts and serve.

Nutritional Analysis: 286 calories, FAT 12 g, PROTEIN 37 g, CARB 9 g, FIBER 5 g, CHOL 87 mg, IRON 6 mg, SODIUM 908 mg, CALC 249 mg

Cooking Lesson

Take care, when cooking chicken breasts, not to overcook. And do try to replace their natural skin coating with something that tastes good, like ball park mustard, which we lay in by the case.

Chicken with a Vinegar Sauce on a Bed of Braised Collard Greens

Talk about an amazing dinner. Picture bright greens nestled under crisp, golden chicken thighs and bathed in a rosy sauce that will make you salute. It's a dinner that combines all those great flavor notes: sweet-and-sour sauce over rich chicken and lovely, bitter greens.

Preparation time: 15 minutes
Cooking time: 25 minutes

MAKES 2 SERVINGS

2 boneless, skinless chicken thighs (10 ounces total)

½ teaspoon kosher salt

½ teaspoon freshly milled black pepper

1 tablespoon unsalted butter

2 garlic cloves, sliced

1 tablespoon finely chopped fresh chives plus additional for garnish

2 tablespoons minced fresh flat-leaf parsley plus additional for garnish

¼ cup red wine vinegar

½ cup low-sodium chicken broth

1 teaspoon tomato paste

2 tablespoons heavy cream

4 cups collard (or other) greens, washed, stemmed, and torn into bite-size pieces

Dry the chicken pieces, then rub with salt and pepper. Heat the butter in a large skillet over medium heat and add the chicken, smooth side down. Brown to a golden color on all sides, about 10 minutes, turning as needed. Add the garlic and brown (don't let it burn) for a minute or two, then add the chives and parsley. Cover the pan, turn the heat to low, and simmer the chicken until cooked through, 15 to 20 minutes. Transfer to a warmed dinner plate.

Raise the heat under the skillet to medium-high. Pour all but 2 tablespoons of fat from the skillet into a medium saucepan (in which you'll cook the greens). Warm the sauce pan over medium-high heat.

Add the vinegar to the skillet, scraping and deglazing it for about 1 minute. Add the broth and tomato paste. Cook and stir until thick, about 5 minutes. Finish with cream and adjust the seasonings with salt and pepper.

Meanwhile, drop greens into hot fat in the saucepan and cook a few moments, then splash in a little sauce from the skillet. Cover and steam a few moments, until the greens are limp but still bright green.

To serve, arrange greens and chicken pieces on a warm dinner plate and slather with rosy, hot sauce. Sprinkle more chives and parsley on top.

Nutritional Analysis: 440 calories, FAT 28 g, PROTEIN 39 g, CARB 8 g, FIBER 3 g, CHOL 171 mg, IRON 3 mg, SODIUM 829 mg, CALC 67 mg

Cooking Lesson

This meal has it all: great flavor, lots of vitamin C in the greens, lots of protein in the chicken. Lots of satisfaction from the combination.

Parmesan-Crusted Chicken with Broccoli Rabe

Italian cooks have been serving chicken cutlets with broccoli rabe for a thousand years. Nobody told them it was good for them. They just liked it. No wonder.

Preparation time: 10 minutes

Cooking time: 25 minutes

MAKES 2 SERVINGS

2 chicken breasts (10 ounces total), split and pounded to ¼-inch thickness

1 tablespoon olive oil

2 tablespoons freshly grated Parmigiano-Reggiano cheese

⅛ teaspoon dried oregano

¼ teaspoon kosher salt

½ teaspoon cayenne

½ cup low-sodium chicken broth

4 cups broccoli rabe

2 garlic cloves, chopped

Fill a 5-quart pot with water and bring to a boil. Preheat the oven to 450°F. Place the chicken in a glass baking dish. Brush both sides with half of the olive oil. In a small bowl, stir together the cheese, oregano, salt, and pepper. Sprinkle over the chicken. Add half the chicken broth, then place in the oven and roast until the chicken is cooked through, about 25 minutes.

When the water comes to a boil, blanch the broccoli rabe pieces for 2 to 3 minutes. This reduces the bitterness. Drain well. Meanwhile, preheat a large skillet over medium-high heat, then film the bottom with the remaining oil. Add the garlic, the blanched broccoli rabe, and the remaining broth, cover, and steam until tender, 5 to 8 minutes.

To serve, divide the broccoli rabe between two dinner plates, and add the chicken cutlets.

Nutritional Analysis: 334 calories, FAT 18 g, PROTEIN 39 g, CARB 9 g, FIBER .16 g, CHOL 92 mg, IRON 2 mg, SODIUM 770 mg, CALC 156 mg

Cooking Lesson

Broccoli rabe is a country cousin to broccoli. Though more bitter, it is, in our opinion, more delectable. You'll recognize it in the case because it has small broccoli crowns along a thick, delicious stem. You cook the whole thing—stems, leaves, and broccoli florets. It is much better if it is blanched prior to sautéing.

Sesame-Crusted Chicken on a Bed of Bean Sprouts

Watch Chinese cooks at the wok, and you'll learn a lot of great techniques for getting maximum flavor from simple ingredients. All you need to complete the meal is a bed of cold raw bean sprouts and you'll get everything in one bite: hot, salty, sweet, bitter, and crunch.

MAKES 2 SERVINGS

Preparation time: 20 minutes

Cooking time: 10 minutes

2 boneless, skinless chicken thighs
  (10 ounces total)

1 teaspoon low sodium soy sauce

1 teaspoon grated fresh ginger

$\frac{1}{2}$ teaspoon ground cinnamon

$\frac{1}{2}$ teaspoon white pepper

$\frac{1}{4}$ teaspoon fennel seeds

$\frac{1}{4}$ teaspoon kosher salt

1 garlic clove, crushed

1 large egg white, lightly beaten

Grated zest from $\frac{1}{2}$ lemon plus 1 teaspoon
  fresh lemon juice

1 tablespoon all-purpose flour

1 tablespoon toasted sesame seeds

2 tablespoons peanut oil

3 cups chilled bean sprouts

Place the thighs in a glass dish. Mix the soy sauce, ginger, cinnamon, white pepper, fennel seeds, salt, and garlic in a small bowl. Pour over the chicken. Cover and set aside for 10 to 15 minutes.

Meanwhile, in a medium bowl, whisk the egg white with the lemon zest and juice until foamy. Sprinkle the chicken pieces with the flour, then dredge in the egg mixture. Preheat a large skillet over medium-high heat, then add the oil. Add the chicken and cook about 6 minutes on each side, or until cooked through.

Divide the bean sprouts between two dinner plates. Top with cooked chicken and serve.

Nutritional Analysis: 396 calories, FAT 19 g, PROTEIN 35 g, CARB 14 g, FIBER 4 g, CHOL 118 mg, IRON 10 mg, SODIUM 538 mg, CALC 50 mg

Cooking Lesson

Use bean sprouts within a day or two of purchasing them. Store, covered, in the refrigerator and rinse well before using.

Chopped Chicken Salad with Romaine

For a great quick meal, start out with ready-roasted chicken breasts from the deli or supermarket.

Preparation time: 10 minutes

MAKES 2 SERVINGS

8 ounces roasted chicken breast, chopped into bite-size pieces

¾ cup chopped red apple (Macintosh or other puckery sweet varieties)

¼ cup chopped celery

1 tablespoon coarsely chopped dry-roasted peanuts

DRESSING

¼ cup plain yogurt

1 tablespoon mayonnaise

½ teaspoon curry powder

¼ teaspoon kosher salt

Pinch of cayenne

4 cups coarsely chopped romaine lettuce leaves

Toss together the chicken, apple, celery, and peanuts in a large bowl. In a small bowl, stir together the ingredients for the dressing. Toss with the chicken mixture. Arrange the lettuce leaves on two plates, mound the chicken mixture on top, and serve.

Nutritional Analysis: 363 calories, FAT 18 g, PROTEIN 39 g, CARB 13 g, FIBER 4 g, CHOL 100 mg, IRON 3 mg, SODIUM 474 mg, CALC 128 mg

Cooking Lesson

We need lots of quick fallback meals to keep us on the carb straight and narrow, and roast chicken from the market is high on our list. You can store the chicken in the refrigerator for several days, and simply cut yourself approximately 1 cup of meat to yield a 4-ounce serving. Go ahead. Eat the skin. That's where the flavor is, and you needn't deprive yourself of it.

Warm Wild Mushroom and Chicken Salad in a Balsamic Vinaigrette

This warm salad will feed your heart and your stomach. The earthy flavor of the mushrooms juxtaposed with the sweet and sour vinaigrette and the bitter greens is delightful. A variety of fresh and rehydrated mushrooms work, including button, morel, cremino, oyster, portobello, and stemmed shiitake.

Preparation time: 15 minutes

Cooking time: 15 minutes

MAKES 2 SERVINGS

2 tablespoons extra-virgin olive oil

1 tablespoon balsamic vinegar

½ teaspoon dried thyme

2 tablespoons finely chopped fresh chives

2 boneless, skinless chicken breasts
(10 ounces total), split and pounded
to ¼-inch thickness

Salt and freshly milled black pepper to taste

½ teaspoon sesame oil

8 ounces assorted wild mushrooms

2 shallots, finely chopped

2 cups mesclun or mixed baby greens

Stir together 2 tablespoons of the olive oil, the vinegar, thyme, and 1 tablespoon of the chives in a medium bowl. Set aside. Toss the chicken breasts with 1 tablespoon of the olive oil and the salt and pepper. Heat a dry medium skillet over medium-high heat for 2 minutes. Add 2 tablespoons of the olive oil and sauté the chicken for 5 to 7 minutes per side, until well done. Add to the bowl of dressing and hold. Toss the mushrooms in the sesame oil and and sauté with the shallots for 3 minutes. Cover and continue to cook for 5 to 7 minutes, stirring occasionally, until the mushrooms are tender. Toss the cooked mushrooms and shallots with the chicken and vinaigrette. Remove the chicken pieces and mushrooms from the dressing and toss in the mesclun greens. Toss thoroughly and divide the greens between two dinner plates, top with the chicken, and then the mushrooms. Garnish with the remaining chives.

Nutritional Analysis: 467 calories, FAT 27 g, PROTEIN 46 g, CARB 11 g, FIBER 3 g,
CHOL 119 mg, IRON 3 mg, SODIUM 709 mg, CALC 63 mg

EGGS: DELICIOUSLY VERSATILE

We love eggs. And the truth is, as long as you have no

identified cholesterol problem, you need not worry about eating them. Eggs are flavorful, fast to prepare, and full of protein, so they fill you up. Recent studies have suggested that eggs provide all nine of the essential amino acids and a host of vitamins not found in the same combination in other foods. Eggs are essential to many dishes and can be a main course. For both Katherine and Linda, they are the emergency dinner of choice. Sauté some scallions, celery, and a bit of fresh dill, whisk in a couple eggs, and you have a satisfyingly quick dinner. You can reduce the saturated fat further by cooking them in olive oil instead of butter.

While there has been altogether too much hype by the media about the dangers of eggs, the food safety issue should be addressed. In fact, salmonella, which is only present on the shell of an egg, is found only on 1 in 10,000 to 1 million eggs, depending on whose statistics you believe. If you get the 1 in

10,000 (you also might win the lottery), it is not likely to multiply in your refrigerator. The biggest risk is in restaurants and institutions serving a big brunch to clientele, when large numbers of eggs are cracked and left out in bowls for hours. In this setting, the raw eggs warm up and provide the perfect environment for pathogens to multiply.

Salmonella inflicts its victims with bad, flulike symptoms but rarely kills anyone. The exceptions are people with compromised immune symptoms, pregnant women (it gravely endangers a fetus), the very old, and the very young. Anyone in one of these groups should avoid food that contains raw or undercooked eggs at all costs. Salmonella in these populations is serious. The list of foods to avoid include any type of mousse, homemade mayonnaise, Caesar salads that use a raw egg yolk, and sunny-side-up or three-minute eggs, to name a few. In our recipes, the eggs are cooked thoroughly.

This delightful protein source is great for fast-lane low-carb eaters. We have developed some voluptuous recipes that prove that eggs are great for dinner. They are also great for lunch and breakfast, and they play an important role in many desserts. If you can buy free-range eggs, do so—they are far superior to pallid, commercially raised eggs. The chickens get out and scratch, eat a few worms, catch a few bugs, and as a result, those yolks are a cheerful yellow, the shells are thicker, and the flavor intensely egg-y. They are still a bargain, even at the higher price.

Crimini Mushrooms and Tomato Frittata

Call it an omelet, a frittata, or an egg pie. The result is the same. If you don't want to stand and cook omelets one at a time, here's the one-dish answer. Load that omelet with good-for-you vegetables (which can be cooked), take your time cutting and cooking them before you add the eggs, and you'll have a one-dish dinner that's satisfying.

Preparation time: 15 minutes
Cooking time: 30 minutes (concurrent)

MAKES 2 SERVINGS

1 tablespoon olive oil
½ cup finely chopped red onion
2 garlic cloves, minced
½ cup chopped red bell pepper
1 cup sliced crimini mushrooms
½ teaspoon kosher salt

½ teaspoon freshly milled black pepper
¼ teaspoon cayenne, or to taste
¼ cup minced plum tomato
6 large eggs
2 tablespoons minced fresh flat-leaf parsley
1 tablespoon chopped fresh chives

Heat a 10-inch ovenproof nonstick skillet over medium heat, then add the oil. One at a time, cut the onion, garlic, bell pepper, and mushrooms and add them to the skillet as you get them cut, stirring after each addition. Season to taste, cover, and cook over medium-low heat until the mushrooms are tender, about 10 minutes. Stir in the tomatoes and cook 5 minutes more.

Whip the eggs in a mixing bowl. Add the parsley and chives and pour over the vegetables. Cook over medium-low heat until the bubbles begin coming up through the bottom and the top is mostly set, about 10 minutes. Run the frittata under the broiler to finish cooking and remove when it's brown and bubbly, about 5 minutes. Cut into wedges and serve warm or at room temperature.

Nutritional Analysis: 328 calories, FAT 22 g, PROTEIN 21 g, CARB 11 g, FIBER 2 g, CHOL 638 Mg, IRON 3 mg, SODIUM 781 mg, CALC 100 mg

Cooking Lesson

Learning to plan your meals is important. Each meal should contain at least 27 grams of protein. Eggs are about 7 grams of protein each. So feel free to add a couple strips bacon (at 4 grams of protein per slice), or sausage (5 grams of protein per patty), or even Canadian bacon (a 2-ounce slice only has 2.5 grams of fat and 12 grams of protein). Then your supper will contain enough protein to hold you until breakfast.

Madras Deviled Eggs

When the English went to India, they combined their favorite foods with those of the natives to create a splendid fusion of East meets West. These hot, frisky deviled eggs can be your Passage to India.

MAKES 2 SERVINGS

Preparation time: 20 minutes

6 large eggs

FILLING

2 tablespoons mayonnaise

1½ tablespoons 2% fat small curd cottage cheese (or ricotta)

1½ teaspoons Madras curry powder

⅛ teaspoon cayenne, or to taste

¼ teaspoon ground cumin

1 tablespoon minced Major Grey's chutney

1 tablespoon chopped fresh chives

Juice of ½ lime

Paprika for dusting the tops of the eggs

½ medium cucumber, peeled

¼ cup rice wine vinegar

½ teaspoon kosher salt

Place the eggs in a medium saucepan and add cold water to cover by at least 1 inch. Bring to a boil over medium-high heat and cook 12 minutes. Run cold water over the eggs to cool, then peel and cut in half.

While the eggs are cooking, mix together the filling ingredients. Mash with the back of a spoon to make a rough puree. Mash the egg yolks into the mixture; then, using a tablespoon or a pastry sleeve, fill the egg whites. Dust with paprika, cover, and refrigerate.

Make a quick pickle by slicing thin ribbons from the cucumber with a potato peeler. Place the cucumber ribbons in a small bowl with rice vinegar, salt, and a few ice cubes. Refrigerate.

Arrange filled eggs on a handsome plate. Drain the cucumbers. Lay cucumber ribbons on top, making accordion ribbons of them for a colorful yellow, green, and white bite.

Nutritional Analysis: 389 calories, FAT 27 g, PROTEIN 22 g, CARB 14 g, FIBER 3 g, CHOL 646 mg, IRON 4 mg, SODIUM 944 mg, CALC 129 mg

Alsatian Cabbage Custard with Country Ham and Goat Cheese

In the South, genteel cooks called this dish "Ladies' Cabbage" because it was considered more refined than the plain, boiled version. In old Texas, the Eckhardt family referred to a particular version of it as *Kohl Kopf,* which translates to "cabbage head." The flavor profile comes from Alsace, that blessed zone between France and Germany which takes the simplest ingredients—including ham, cabbage, eggs, and local cheeses—and forges them into haute cuisine, or at least "faux Haute."

Preparation time: 5 minutes
Cooking time: 35 minutes

Call it what you will, this multilayered dish gives you plenty of flavor and texture. We call this Saturday cooking because it takes 30 minutes just to bake the cabbage custard, but it's worth the wait. You could double this recipe and serve it to guests, who would drop their forks. It's that good.

Don't be put off by the long list of ingredients and the work instructions. It's not that difficult. First prepare and bake the cabbage. While it's baking, wrap thin ham slices around goat cheese disks, slather with mustard, and wait. All you're going to do with them is place them atop the cabbage to heat through. During that same 30 minutes, make the sauce, which will add a four-star finish to this lovely dinner. You'll get an explosion of pleasing tastes and textures, and an aroma that will set your mouth watering before you've taken the first bite.

MAKES 2 SERVINGS

2 cups shredded green cabbage

2 teaspoons unsalted butter

¼ cup shredded shallots

½ cup milk

1 large egg plus 2 egg yolks

⅛ teaspoon Tabasco sauce

½ teaspoon salt

½ teaspoon freshly milled black pepper

3 ounces thinly sliced prosciutto or country
   ham

2 ounces goat cheese cut into 4 disks

1 teaspoon Dijon mustard

SAUCE

2 tablespoons chopped celery

1 tablespoon Madeira

2 tablespoons water or chicken broth

2 tablespoons cream

½ teaspoon salt

½ teaspoon freshly milled black pepper, or to
   taste

Place a baking pan half full of water in the oven for a water bath. Heat the oven to 325°F. Butter a 3-cup baking dish. Fill a medium saucepan with water and bring to a boil. Butter a piece of wax paper large enough to cover the baking dish.

Drop the cabbage into the boiling water and blanch for 1 minute, then drain. Heat 1 teaspoon of the butter in a medium skillet, then add 1 tablespoon of the shallots and sauté for 30 seconds. Stir in the cabbage and sauté until the cabbage begins to brown, about 3 minutes.

Whisk together the milk, egg, egg yolks, Tabasco, salt, and pepper in a mixing bowl. Transfer the cabbage to the prepared baking dish. Pour the milk and egg mixture over the cabbage. Cover with the buttered wax paper and place in the hot water bath in the oven. Bake 30 minutes.

While the custard cooks, prepare the ham packets. Lay 2 ham slices in a cross pattern, then top with a disk of goat cheese. Fold the ham until you have a neat package with no cheese visible. Repeat with the remaining ham and goat cheese. Slather the tops with Dijon mustard. After the cabbage has cooked for 30 minutes, remove the wax paper and slip the ham packets atop the cabbage. Cook 5 more minutes before serving.

Meanwhile, in the skillet you used to sauté the cabbage, melt the second teaspoon of butter. Sauté the remaining shallots and the celery for 2 minutes, stirring. Then add Madeira and water or broth stirring to lift the browned bits off the bottom of the skillet. Boil a minute or so, then stir in the cream and season to taste with salt and pepper.

Pour the sauce over the top of the baked custard and serve at once.

Nutritional Analysis: 374 calories, FAT 24 g, PROTEIN 24 g, CARB 13 g, FIBER 2 g, CHOL 283 mg, IRON 3 mg, SODIUM 2,013 mg, CALC 200 mg

Cooking Lesson

This menu was inspired by a visit to Larry Forgione's fine midtown Manhattan restaurant, An American Place. Larry is a master of layering flavors, creating dishes that look good and taste good. Eat with him, and you'll develop great standards. Now about that dessert menu. Just smile and say "Espresso, please," when the time comes.

Menu Suggestion

A plate of cantaloupe and shards of blue cheese will finish this meal perfectly.

Shirred Eggs Florentine

Quick as a wink, this latter-day Popeye supper is satisfying and easy to put together after work. Just remember to turn the oven on to 350°F before you even open the refrigerator door to snatch up the eggs.

Preparation time: 5 minutes
Baking time: 20 to 25 minutes

MAKES 2 SERVINGS

One 12-ounce box chopped frozen spinach, thawed, or 1 pound fresh baby spinach wilted (see note)

2 scallions, white and green parts, thinly sliced

½ cup light cream

2 tablespoons grated Parmesan cheese

2 tablespoons grated mozzarella cheese

½ teaspoon freshly grated nutmeg

¼ teaspoon kosher salt

½ teaspoon freshly milled black pepper

4 large eggs

2 tablespoons chopped hazelnuts

Heat the oven to 350° F. Lightly butter a 7 × 10-inch baking dish or two 6-inch ramekins. Arrange the spinach in the dish(es). Using the back of a large spoon, make indentations in the spinach. Put the cream in a small bowl and mix with grated cheeses, nutmeg, salt, and pepper. Then, pour around the spinach. Break the eggs into the indentations. Sprinkle hazelnuts on top, then bake 20 to 25 minutes, or until the egg whites are set, but the yolks are still soft. Serve hot.

Nutritional Analysis: 398 calories, FAT 30 g, PROTEIN 23 g, CARB 12 g, FIBER 5 g, CHOL 473 mg, IRON 4 mg, SODIUM 692 mg, CALC 430 mg

Cooking Lesson

Use fresh baby spinach if you wish. It will take 5 minutes longer to prepare than frozen spinach, but you'll get a bright green and the freshest taste ever. Buy a pound of it, bring it home, and wash it, spinning it dry. Then wilt it in an ovenproof skillet or gratin dish over high heat, tossing just until the spinach collapses. Now, drain the liquid and proceed with the recipe, making indentations in the spinach and breaking the eggs into them.

Health Benefit

Spinach is, as Popeye knew, good for you, has plenty of iron, lots of fiber, and tastes good besides.

Poached Eggs with Lime-Jalapeño Hollandaise Sauce on a Bed of Roasted Yellow Crookneck Squash

The lime-jalapeño combination spruces up this classic recipe, which is made in the microwave. Once you have made hollandaise in the microwave, you will never go back to the stove-top method.

MAKES 2 SERVINGS

HOLLANDAISE SAUCE

¼ cup (½ stick) unsalted butter

2 large egg yolks

1 tablespoon fresh lime juice

½ teaspoon finely chopped lime zest

½ jalapeño, seeded and finely chopped

4 large eggs

Salt and freshly milled black pepper to taste

Roasted Yellow Squash with Lemon Juice
    (page 23)

Melt the butter in the microwave on high (100 percent power) for 1 minute in a small bowl. Whisk together the egg yolks, lime juice, lime zest, and jalapeño in a medium bowl. Dribble the melted butter into the egg mixture very slowly, whisking constantly, leaving the foamy milk solids at the bottom of the bowl in which the butter was melted; discard the solids. Return the sauce to the microwave and cook on medium (55 percent power) for 30 seconds. Whisk vigorously as the sauce thickens. The whisk should leave a track in the sauce. You may need to cook it for 30 seconds more at medium (50 percent power), depending on the strength of your microwave.

Be careful not to overcook the sauce, or the egg yolks will curdle. (If they do curdle, you can sometimes save a hollandaise by stirring in an ice cube.) Keep warm.

Bring water to a boil in an egg-poaching pan. Butter the poaching cups and break the eggs into the cups. Cook for 4 minutes (for a runny yolk) or to the desired degree of doneness. Gently place an egg over each serving of roasted squash and top with some hollandaise. Serve at once.

Nutritional Analysis, including the squash: 385 calories, FAT 35 g, PROTEIN 14 g, CARB 3 g, FIBER .06 g, CHOL 591 mg, IRON 2 mg, SODIUM 330 mg, CALC 72 mg

Egg and White Wine Sauce

This lovely yellow sauce is a no-nonsense New England cousin to hollandaise. It tastes so good that it will liven up any number of boring, bland diet entrées: the ubiquitous chicken breast, steamed fish, cauliflower. Here we have paired the sauce with eggs cooked over easy and perched on pureed cauliflower. The sauce will keep in the refrigerator for 3 days, so keep some on hand.

MAKES 2 SERVINGS

Preparation time: 15 minutes
Cooking time: 6 minutes

⅓ cup chopped onion

¼ cup dry white wine

½ cup half-and-half

¼ cup (½ stick) unsalted butter, softened

Zest and juice of ½ lemon

½ teaspoon kosher salt

½ teaspoon freshly milled black pepper

4 large eggs, cooked over easy

Cauliflower Purée (page 164)

Finely chopped fresh flat-leaf parsley for
   garnish

Combine the onion and wine in a saucepan and cook over medium-high heat until reduced by three-quarters and the liquid is nearly evaporated. Add the half-and-half and boil to reduce by about a third. Turn off the heat and whisk in the butter. Add the lemon juice and zest, and salt and pepper. Set aside and keep warm.

   Cook the eggs in a sauté pan filmed with butter over medium heat, turning once. Lay the eggs over the puréed cauliflower and top with the sauce. Garnish with chopped parsley.

Nutritional Analysis: 346 calories, FAT 33 g, PROTEIN 7 g, CARB 3 g, FIBER .2 g,
CHOL 292 mg, IRON .9 mg, SODIUM 567 mg, CALC 70 mg

Green Olive and Yellow Onion Tortilla

The Spanish live on *tortillas,* cousins to Italian frittatas that are especially good after a hard day's work. This recipe skips the potato, traditionally the basis for a tortilla.

MAKES 2 SERVINGS

Preparation time: 15 minutes

Cooking time: 15 minutes (concurrent)

1 tablespoon olive oil

½ cup yellow onion, coarsely chopped

2 garlic cloves, minced

½ cup chopped green olives

½ teaspoon Kosher salt

½ teaspoon freshly milled black pepper

¼ cup minced fresh plum tomato

½ cup minced flat leaf parsley plus
   2 tablespoons for garnish

½ teaspoon paprika

6 large eggs

Heat a 10-inch nonstick skillet over medium heat, then add the oil. Add the onions, garlic, and green olives, stirring after each additon. Season with the salt and pepper, reduce the heat to medium-low heat, and cook until the onions are translucent, about 7 minutes. Stir in the tomatoes and parsley and cook 3 minutes more.

Beat the eggs with the paprika and pour over the vegetables. Cook over medium-low heat until bubbles begin coming up through the bottom and the top is mostly set, about 10 minutes. Run the tortilla under the broiler to finish cooking and remove when it's brown and bubbly, about 5 minutes. Cut into wedges and serve with the reserved chopped parsley.

Nutritional Analysis: 348 calories, FAT 26 g, PROTEIN 20 g, CARB 9 g, FIBER .2 g,
CHOL 637 mg, IRON 4 mg, SODIUM 460 mg, CALC 129 mg

THE EXTRAS: VINAIGRETTES, DRESSINGS, DRY RUBS, AND MARINADES

Keeping salads interesting isn't hard, it just takes a
few good recipes. We have given you a wide range, from classics to off-the-
wall options. Use these recipes as springboards to make up your own
concoctions.

Whizzing up homemade salad dressing is economical and gives you
more flavor options. We often make the vinaigrettes and dressing right in the
bottom of the salad bowl to minimize clean-ups. After the dressing is made,
layer the vegetables on top of the dressing, then toss just before serving.
Cover and refrigerate up to four hours to keep the salad from becoming soggy.
This method has the desirable effect of marinating the ingredients that are
resting in the dressing while leaving those on top crisp. When you mix the

marinated greens or vegetables throughout the rest of the salad just before serving, the result is outstanding.

Each of these recipes makes about 3 tablespoons of salad dressing, plenty for two (or even four) servings if you toss the salad thoroughly. A little elbow grease in tossing salad will cut your calorie count in half. You may even find that you can get away with using less. If so, go for it. (Never miss an opportunity to save calories!)

Finally, we also believe that these salad dressings are great for more than just salad greens. They can be used for marinating meat before it is cooked. (Always discard any marinade that has had raw meat in it.) These dressings will improve the flavor of blanched and steamed vegetables as well. Use the same bottom-of-the-bowl method described above, add your crisp-cooked veggies, toss, and enjoy.

Egg and Lemon Sauce

If the question "Which came first, the chicken or the egg?" ever crossed your mind, this sauce will provide the answer. A no-nonsense New England cousin to hollandaise, it tastes so good that it will enliven any number of boring, bland diet entrées: the ubiquitous chicken breast, steamed fish, or cauliflower. Make it and keep it on hand. To stay on your diet, you need all the help you can get. Here it is—in a jar.

Preparation time: 15 minutes
Cooking time: 6 minutes

MAKES 24 (1-TABLESPOON) SERVINGS

4 large eggs

4 scallions, white and green parts, minced

½ cup dry white wine

1 cup light cream

1 cup (2 sticks) unsalted butter, softened

Grated zest and juice of 1 lemon

½ teaspoon kosher salt

½ teaspoon freshly milled black pepper

¼ cup chopped fresh flat-leaf parsley

Cook the eggs in boiling in water to cover until hard cooked, about 6 minutes. Combine the scallions and wine in a saucepan and boil down until the liquid is nearly evaporated, about 2 minutes. Add the cream and boil to reduce by about a third. Off the heat, whisk in the butter, then add the lemon zest and juice, salt, and pepper.

Peel the eggs and chop. Add to the sauce with the parsley. Keep warm over indirect heat or transfer to a jar, cover, and refrigerate up to 1 week.

Nutritional Analysis: 135 calories, FAT 11.3 g, PROTEIN 1.4 g, CARB 1.4 g, FIBER 0.2 g, CHOL 57 mg, IRON .75 mg, SODIUM 140 mg, CALC 27 mg

White Wine Vinegar and Walnut Vinaigrette

This bracing vinaigrette is great over beets, avocado slices, spinach leaves, or grilled meats as well as plain old greens. In fact, you might want to just eat it with a spoon!

Preparation time: 5 minutes

MAKES 2 SERVINGS

2 tablespoon white wine vinegar

½ teaspoon Dijon mustard

2 tablespoons walnut oil (see note)

1 tablespoon finely chopped walnuts

Salt and freshly milled black pepper to taste

Mix all of the ingredients in a salad bowl. Taste and adjust the seasoning. Layer in the greens, cover and refrigerate until meal time, and toss just before serving. Alternatively, drizzle the vinaigrette over chopped vegetables.

NOTE: Walnut oil is available at gourmet stores and better grocery stores. For a little variety, walnut oil is an earthy alternative to olive oil. If you don't already love it, you will learn to! Buy the smallest amount possible and store it in the refrigerator after you open it, as it has a short shelf life.

Nutritional Analysis: 144 calories, FAT 16 g, PROTEIN 1 g, CARB 1 g, FIBER .3 g,
CHOL 0 mg, IRON .3 mg, SODIUM 615 mg, CALC 8 mg

Garlic Ranch-Style Dressing

This creamy salad dressing enhances spinach-based salads in a voluptuous way.

Preparation time: 5 minutes

MAKES 2 SERVINGS

1 teaspoon garlic powder

2 tablespoons mayonnaise

2 teaspoons Dijon mustard

2 tablespoons fresh lemon juice

Salt and freshly milled black pepper to taste

Mix all of the ingredients in a salad bowl. Toss with a salad and serve.

Nutritional Analysis: 129 calories, FAT 13 g, PROTEIN 2 g, CARB 5 g, FIBER 1 g,
CHOL 7 mg, IRON 1 mg, SODIUM 1,041 mg, CALC 29 mg

Red Onion and Cilantro Dressing

This spicy blend zips up fruit and lettuce salad or even bitter greens.

Preparation time: 5 minutes

SERVES 2

1 teaspoon finely chopped red onion

½ teaspoon finely chopped crystallized ginger

1 tablespoon blanched and slivered almonds

2 teaspoons sesame seeds

¼ teaspoon anise seed

1 teaspoon minced fresh cilantro

⅛ teaspoon cayenne

1 tablespoon white wine vinegar

1 tablespoon extra-virgin olive oil

In a small bowl, combine the onion, ginger, almonds, sesame seeds, anise seed, cilantro, cayenne, and vinegar. Stir in the olive oil until well combined.

Nutritional Analysis: 108 calories, FAT 9 g, PROTEIN 4 g, CARB 5 g, FIBER 2 g,
CHOL 0 mg, IRON 1 mg, SODIUM 2 mg, CALC 80 mg

Dilly Ranch Creamed Dressing

Cabbage-based salads come alive with a dose of this dill-flavored dressing. Once you get used to using fresh dill, you will never return to the dried stuff!

MAKES 2 SERVINGS

Preparation time: 5 minutes

2 tablespoons mayonnaise

1 tablespoon finely chopped fresh dill

1 tablespoon white wine vinegar

1 teaspoon Dijon mustard

Stir together all of the ingredients in a salad bowl. Toss with salad and serve.

Nutritional Analysis: 103 calories, FAT 11 g, PROTEIN .4 g, CARB .4 g, FIBER 0 g, CHOL 7 mg, IRON 0 mg, SODIUM 144 mg, CALC 7 mg

Hot Cha Cha Salad Dressing

Drizzle this dressing over wedges of iceberg lettuce with grated mild Cheddar cheese on top—think of it as a sort of retro Tex Mex salad.

Preparation time: 5 minutes

MAKES 2 SERVINGS

1 tablespoon extra-virgin olive oil

1 tablespoon mayonnaise

2 tablespoons mild or hot salsa

¼ teaspoon freshly milled black pepper

⅛ teaspoon ground cumin

1 teaspoon garlic powder

¼ teaspoon oregano

Cayenne to taste (optional)

Salt and freshly milled black pepper to taste

Mix all of the ingredients thoroughly in a small bowl. Taste and adjust seasonings.

Nutritional Analysis: 126 calories, FAT 13 g, PROTEIN .5 g, CARB 3 g, FIBER 1 g, CHOL 3 mg, IRON 0 mg, SODIUM 737 mg, CALC 10 mg

Cajun-Style Vinaigrette

This vinaigrette kicks up greens or a chopped vegetable salad, such as beets or red peppers.

MAKES 2 SERVINGS

Preparation time: 5 minutes

2 tablespoons red wine vinegar

$\frac{1}{2}$ teaspoon sweet paprika

$\frac{1}{2}$ teaspoon grainy Dijon mustard

$\frac{1}{8}$ teaspoon cayenne or to taste

$\frac{1}{8}$ teaspoon (or less) sugar substitute, optional or to taste

2 tablespoons extra-virgin olive oil

Salt and freshly milled black pepper to taste

Stir together all of the ingredients in a salad bowl. Taste and adjust seasonings. Layer salad greens on top, toss, and serve.

Nutritional Analysis: 125 calories, FAT 14 g, PROTEIN .2 g, CARB 2 g, FIBER .4 g, CHOL 0 mg, IRON 0 mg, SODIUM 613 mg, CALC 6.1 mg

Basic Mustard Vinaigrette

This is a classic and an old standby in our house. It is especially good on bitter greens.

Preparation time: 5 minutes

MAKES 2 SERVINGS

2 tablespoons extra-virgin olive oil

2 teaspoons grainy mustard

1 tablespoon garlic powder

½ teaspoon prepared horseradish

2 tablespoons red wine vinegar

¼ teaspoon sugar

Salt and freshly milled black pepper to taste

Mix all of the ingredients in a salad bowl. Taste and adjust seasonings. Layer with the salad greens and toss just before serving.

Nutritional Analysis: 135 calories, FAT 14 g, PROTEIN .6 g, CARB 4 g, FIBER 1 g, CHOL 0 mg, IRON .3 mg, SODIUM 665 mg, CALC 11 mg

Ginger and Red Hot Pepper Vinaigrette

Cabbage and basic salad greens alike get a lift from this spicy
Asian-inspired dressing.

Preparation time: 5 minutes

MAKES 2 SERVINGS

1 tablespoon rice wine vinegar

¼ teaspoon sugar

1 garlic clove, finely chopped

½ teaspoon finely chopped fresh ginger

¼ teaspoon crushed dried hot chiles

¼ teaspoon dry mustard

¼ teaspoon sesame oil

2 tablespoons vegetable oil

Mix all of the ingredients in a salad bowl. Taste and adjust seasonings. Layer with salad greens
and toss just before serving.

Nutritional Analysis: 131 calories, FAT 14 g, PROTEIN .2 g, CARB 1 g, FIBER 0 g,
CHOL 0 mg, IRON 0 mg, SODIUM 16 mg, CALC 4 mg

Sesame-Miso Vinaigrette

Miso is fermented soy paste and is believed to aid digestion. It can be found at any Asian market and at many grocery stores. Try this sauce with sturdy greens and firm vegetables like cucumbers or radishes.

Preparation time: 5 minutes

MAKES 2 SERVINGS

2 tablespoons extra-virgin olive oil

1 teaspoon dark sesame oil

3 tablespoons rice wine vinegar

1 teaspoon golden miso

1 teaspoon sugar

1 teaspoon minced fresh ginger

Salt and freshly milled black pepper to taste

Stir together all of the ingredients in a salad bowl. Taste and adjust seasonings. Layer salad greens on top of the dressing. Toss just before serving.

Nutritional Analysis: 155 calories, FAT 16 g, PROTEIN .4 g, CARB 3 g, FIBER .32 g, CHOL 0 mg, IRON 0 mg, SODIUM 686 mg, CALC 5 mg

Three-Citrus Vinaigrette

Preparation time: 5 minutes

1 tablespoon fresh lemon juice

1 tablespoon fresh lime juice

1 tablespoon fresh orange juice

1 teaspoon rice wine vinegar

3 tablespoons extra-virgin olive oil

½ teaspoon sugar

Salt and freshly milled black pepper to taste

Mix all of the ingredients in a large salad bowl. Layer lettuce leaves onto the dressing. Toss just before serving.

Nutritional Analysis: 101 calories, FAT 20 g, PROTEIN .1 g, CARB 0 g, FIBER .1 g,
CHOL 0 mg, IRON 0 mg, SODIUM 290 mg, CALC 2.3 mg

ABOUT DRY RUBS

Every cuisine has dry rubs in some form or another, even Texas barbecue always starts with a dry rub. Unlike using a wet marinade, rubbing a piece of meat with dry spices before cooking means you can sear the meat properly, thus locking in the juices. A liquid sauce is good for glazing a piece of meat after it has been seared and during the last 15 minutes of cooking time. Sauces are also good for dipping after the meat has been cooked.

Every high-protein cook should have a few dry rubs in his or her bag of kitchen tricks. They add big flavor while adding only a negligible number of carbohydrates, and if you make them up in advance, they are convenient, too. The lack of time to cook, think about cooking, or even eat is one of the primary reasons we let our diets get out of control.

Ready-mixed dry rubs are becoming available in many of the better grocery stores, but they're so easy to make, why go to the expense? We offer you a dozen that you can make up in advance and keep on hand for an emergency dinner. Take an evening, put on some CDs, and bottle yourself at least a couple of different dry rubs. Label them clearly, and even jot down on the label what to spread them on. This is one of those stitch-in-time activities that you will come to appreciate on many occasions. You can go two weeks without repeating the same flavor combo with these additions to your pantry. And we encourage you to develop your own secret dry rubs.

Because the calories and carb count for each of these dry rubs (serving size is about ½ teaspoon) is negligble, use them any time.

How to Use a Dry Rub

As soon as you get the meat or fish out of the refrigerator, pat it dry of its own juices and *rub* (not sprinkle) the meat on both sides with 1 teaspoon of dry rub per pound of meat, chicken, fish, etc. Pretty simple, really. Let the meat rest while you prep the other ingredients and dishes. Then just grill or broil. For extra flavor, you can rub the meat with a little olive oil or lemon juice. This is especially good for very lean cuts of meat and fish.

White Pepper and Clove Dry Rub

White pepper and cloves combine to perfume any meat nicely.
Try it on fish, chicken, veal, and pork.

Preparation time: 5 minutes

MAKES ABOUT ½ CUP

¼ cup white peppercorns

1 tablespoon ground allspice

1 tablespoon ground cinnamon

1 tablespoon ground savory

2 tablespoons whole cloves

2 tablespoons ground nutmeg

2 tablespoons paprika

2 tablespoons dried thyme

Combine all of the ingredients in a blender or food processor. Store in a jar with a tight-fitting lid.

Nutritional Analysis: 12 calories, FAT 1 g, PROTEIN .2 g, CARB 2 g, FIBER 1 g,
CHOL 0 mg, IRON 1 mg, SODIUM 3 mg, CALC 24 mg

Chili Dry Rub

This dry rub is a standby in our homes. Fast and flavorful, it really goes with anything: pork, chicken, steaks, even salmon steaks.

MAKES ABOUT ¹⁄₂ CUP

Preparation time: 5 minutes

2 tablespoons garlic powder

3 tablespoons paprika

1 tablespoon chili powder

2 teaspoons salt

1 teaspoon freshly milled black pepper, or to taste

¹⁄₄ teaspoon cayenne

Grind the spice mixture in a food processor or blender, or use a mortar and pestle. Store in a jar with a tight-fitting lid.

Nutritional Analysis: 22 calories, FAT .5 g, PROTEIN 1 g, CARB 4 g, FIBER 1 g, CHOL 0 mg, IRON 1 mg, SODIUM 593 mg, CALC 11 mg

Bourbon Street Spice Blend

This goes on pork and chicken, shrimp and crab, and, of course, crayfish. Play some jazz and spice up a meal.

MAKES ABOUT ¹/₂ CUP

Preparation time: 5 minutes

2 tablespoons paprika

1 tablespoon cayenne

1 tablespoon dry mustard

2 teaspoons salt

2 teaspoons freshly milled black pepper

2 teaspoons garlic powder

2 teaspoons ground sage

1 teaspoon white pepper

1 teaspoon onion powder

1 teaspoon ground cumin

1 teaspoon dried thyme

1 teaspoon dried oregano

Mix all of the ingredients in a small bowl. Store in a jar with a tight-fitting lid.

Nutritional Analysis: 22 calories, FAT .9 g, PROTEIN 1 g, CARB 3 g, FIBER 1 g,
CHOL 0 mg, IRON 1 mg, SODIUM 583 mg, CALC 25 mg

Homemade Curry Powder

Curry spice blends are found in cuisines ranging from Africa to Korea. Once you get used to the idea of mixing your own curry, you won't go back to the store-bought variety, which often has too much celery seed and salt. Keep this on hand and customize it when you season your food, adding more of whatever spice you want to be more prominent. Trial and error will teach you what is good. That way, no curry dish you make will taste the same! This is good on fish, chicken, lamb, and vegetables.

MAKES ABOUT ½ CUP

Preparation time: 5 minutes

3 tablespoons ground coriander

2 tablespoons ground cumin

1½ tablespoons turmeric

1 tablespoon ground cloves

2 teaspoons ground cinnamon

2 teaspoons ground nutmeg

1½ teaspoons ground cardamom

1¼ teaspoons ground ginger

1 teaspoon freshly milled black pepper

1 teaspoon cayenne

In a small bowl, mix all of the ingredients. Store in a jar with a tight-fitting lid.

Nutritional Analysis: 18 calories, FAT 1 g, PROTEIN 1 g, CARB 3 g, FIBER 1 g, CHOL 0 mg, IRON 2 mg, SODIUM 6 mg, CALC 32 mg

Basic Jerk Seasoning

The flavors of the Caribbean will make any diner at your table happy. Try it on chicken, pork, and beef.

Preparation time: 5 minutes

MAKES ABOUT ¹/₂ CUP

1 tablespoon onion powder

1 tablespoon ground allspice

1 tablespoon freshly milled black pepper

1 tablespoon cayenne

1 tablespoon garlic powder

1 teaspoon dried thyme

1 teaspoon ground cinnamon

¹/₂ teaspoon habanero chile powder

¹/₂ teaspoon ground nutmeg

2 bay leaves

1 tablespoon salt

1 teaspoon sugar

Grind up all ingredients in a food processor or blender. Store in a jar with a tight-fitting lid.

Nutritional Analysis: 16 calories, FAT .3 g, PROTEIN .5 g, CARB 4 g, FIBER 1 g, CHOL 0 mg, IRON 1 mg, SODIUM 874 mg, CALC 22 mg

Louisiana Swampland Dry Rub

Put a little BAM in your dinner with this Cajun spice rub. It will heat up any meal. It is especially good on pork, chicken. shrimp, and crab. Keep it on hand for those nights you have a craving for something down and dirty with a real bite.

MAKES ABOUT ¾ CUP

Preparation time: 5 minutes

2 tablespoons garlic powder

2 tablespoons paprika

2 tablespoons dried oregano

2 tablespoons dried thyme

1 tablespoon freshly milled black pepper

1 tablespoon onion powder

1 teaspoon cayenne (or as much as you can take)

1 teaspoon salt

Grind up all ingredients in a blender or food processor. Store in a jar with a tight-fitting lid.

Nutritional Analysis: 17 calories, FAT .4 g, PROTEIN .7 g, CARB 4 g, FIBER 1 g, CHOL 0 mg, IRON 1.6 mg, SODIUM 180 mg, CALC 31 mg

North African Spice Rub

Katherine got this from a friend who has traveled extensively in Tunisia and Morocco. The ingredient list may be intimidating, but once you have it on hand you won't want to live without it. Try it on salmon, chicken, beef, and lamb.

Preparation time: 5 minutes

MAKES ABOUT 1/2 CUP

1 tablespoon ground cardamom

1 tablespoon ground cinnamon

2 teaspoons ground nutmeg

1 1/2 teaspoons turmeric

1 teaspoon ground cloves

1 teaspoon ground ginger

1 teaspoon ground cumin

1 teaspoon cayenne

1 teaspoon ground coriander

1/2 teaspoon lavender

1/2 teaspoon fennel seed

1 teaspoon salt

Grind up all of the ingredients in a food processor or with a mortal and pestle. Store in a jar with a tight-fitting lid.

Nutritional Analysis: 17 calories, FAT 7 g, PROTEIN 4 g, CARB 3 g, FIBER 2 g, CHOL 0 mg, IRON 1 mg, SODIUM 390 mg, CALC 27 mg

Gordon's Super Fast Spice Rub

Ever heard the saying, "The cobbler has no shoes"? Well, the same saying can be applied to a cookbook writer's family, only meals are what's missing. Here is a solution that Katherine's husband came up with for the ubiquitous pork chops and chicken thighs that they keep in the freezer for emergency dinners. Gordon discovered that this blend is even good on eggs and cottage cheese. Rub it on chicken, pork, veal, fish, and beef.

MAKES ABOUT ¼ CUP

Preparation time: 5 minutes

2 tablespoons adobo seasoning (see note)

2 tablespoons five-spice powder (see note)

1 teaspoon salt

Freshly milled black pepper to taste.

Mix all of the ingredients together. Store in a jar with a tight-fitting lid.

NOTE: Five-spice powder is available in Asian groceries; adobo seasoning is found in the Hispanic section of most supermarkets.

Nutritional Analysis: 16 calories, FAT 1 g, PROTEIN 1 g, CARB 3 g, FIBER 2 g, CHOL 0 mg, IRON 1 mg, SODIUM 438 mg, CALC 15 mg

Texas Big Flavor Rub

Like many things Texan, this rub delivers a big flavor. Unlike other parts of the South, Texans rarely use sugar in their spice mixtures. This one is especially good on beef (naturally)! It's great on chicken, pork, and salmon steaks, too.

MAKES ABOUT 1 CUP

Preparation time: 5 minutes

¼ **cup salt**

¼ **cup paprika**

¼ **cup chili powder**

3 **tablespoons freshly milled black pepper**

2 **tablespoons garlic powder**

1 **tablespoon ground cumin**

2 **teaspoons cayenne**

Combine all of the ingredients in a small bowl. Store in a jar with a tight-fitting lid.

Nutritional Analysis: 16 calories, FAT 1 g, PROTEIN 1 g, CARB 3 g, FIBER 1 g, CHOL 0 mg, IRON 1 mg, SODIUM 1,764 mg, CALC 18 mg

Clove and Paprika Dry Rub

Don't be intimidated by the long list of spices. For those days when you need something fast and good and *different,* this works wonders on fish, fowl, pork, or beef. It even goes on some puréed vegetable, like cauliflower or fennel.

MAKES ABOUT 1 CUP

Preparation time: 5 minutes

2 bay leaves

2 tablespoons ground cloves

2 tablespoons ground nutmeg

2 tablespoons sweet Hungarian paprika

2 tablespoons dried thyme

1 tablespoon ground allspice

5 tablespoons ground white pepper

1 teaspoon salt

Mix the ingredients together in a shallow bowl. Store in a jar with a tight-fitting lid.

Nutritional Analysis: 18 calories, FAT 1 g, PROTEIN 1 g, CARB 4 g, FIBER 2 g,
CHOL 0 mg, IRON 2 mg, SODIUM 149 mg, CALC 32 mg

Parsley, Sage, Rosemary, and Thyme Dry Rub

The flavors of this rub are subtle and excellent for sautéing, grilling, baking, or braising chicken or fish.

MAKES ABOUT ³⁄₄ CUP

Preparation time: 5 minutes

¼ cup onion powder

¼ cup paprika

1 tablespoon ground black pepper

½ teaspoon cayenne

1 tablespoon dried parsley

1 tablespoon dried sage

1 tablespoon crumbled rosemary

1 tablespoon dried thyme

Combine all of the ingredients in a blender or food processor. Store in a jar with a tight-fitting lid.

Nutritional Analysis: 16 calories, FAT .4 g, PROTEIN 1 g, CARB 3 g, FIBER 1 g,
CHOL 0 mg, IRON 1 mg, SODIUM 2 mg, CALC 25 mg

Taos Mountain Chipolte Rub

Katherine and Gordon have spent many wonderful Christmases on Taos Mountain. Here is a recipe a local shared with them. It is great on chicken, veal, pork, and beef as well as on freshly roasted corn and on cucumbers.

Preparation time: 5 minutes

MAKES ABOUT 1 CUP

5 dried chipotle chiles

5 dried ancho chiles

½ cup garlic powder

¼ cup dried oregano

2 tablespoons salt

Mix together all ingredients in a blender or food processor. Store in a jar with a tight-fitting lid.

Nutritional Analysis: 23 calories, FAT .4 g, PROTEIN 1 g, CARB 5 g, FIBER 2 g, CHOL 0 mg, IRON 1 mg, SODIUM 875 mg, CALC 25 mg

Ginger and Clove Dry Rub

Here is a spicy variation on the theme that's especially good on chicken, fish, and lamb, though it works for pork and beef, too.

Preparation time: 5 minutes

MAKES ABOUT ¾ CUP

6 tablespoons ground ginger

3 tablespoons garlic powder

3 tablespoons paprika

3 tablespoons dried thyme

1 tablespoon ground celery seed

1 teaspoon ground cloves

1 teaspoon salt

1 teaspoon freshly milled black pepper

Pinch of cayenne

Combine all of the ingredients in a small bowl. Store in a jar with a tight-fitting lid.

Nutritional Analysis: 20 calories, FAT .5 g, PROTEIN 1 g, CARB 4 g, FIBER 1 g, CHOL 0 mg, IRON 2 mg, SODIUM 169 mg, CALC 33 mg

Mexican Mint Rub

Choose this Mexican rub for lamb or fish. Heightened the flavor each time you use it by rubbing the meat with lemon juice just before adding the dry rub.

Preparation time: 5 minutes

MAKES ABOUT 1 CUP

½ cup dried mint leaves

¼ cup onion powder

2 tablespoons salt

2 teaspoons ground coriander

2 teaspoons freshly milled black pepper

1 teaspoon ground allspice

Combine all ingredients in a blender of food processor. Store in a jar with a tight-fitting lid.

Nutritional Analysis: 14 calories, FAT .1 g, PROTEIN 1 g, CARB 3 g, FIBER 1 g, CHOL 0 mg, IRON 4 mg, SODIUM 881 mg, CALC 44 mg

THE SIDES: SALSAS, SLAWS, CHUTNEYS, SALADS, AND PURÉES

For us, one of the keys to staying on

any regimen, be it diet, exercise, or anything, is fighting boredom. To keep high-protein meals interesting, it is important to branch out from steamed broccoli and spinach. Here are a dozen of our favorite combos that help us avoid bland steamed veggies! All of these accompaniments go together quickly, use bright flavors and colors, and have a great texture.

What we have tried to do is to combine simple flavors, textures, and beautiful colors for smashing results. We hope you will use these assorted side dishes as a guide and begin to create your own.

Celery, Black Olive, and Caper Salsa

This salad is salty, crunchy, and sour all at once. The green celery is beautiful against the black olives. Serve with beef, chicken, or fish.

Preparation time: 15 minutes

MAKES 2 SERVINGS

1 tablespoon fresh lemon juice

2 tablespoons red wine vinegar

3 tablespoons extra-virgin olive oil

¾ cup coarsely chopped celery

½ cup black olives, pitted and sliced

2 tablespoons drained capers

¼ cup chopped fresh flat-leaf parsley

Salt and freshly milled black pepper to taste

In a medium bowl, combine the lemon juice, red wine vinegar, and olive oil. Toss in the celery, olives, capers, and parsley. Taste and add salt and pepper as needed. Chill until just before serving.

Nutritional Analysis: 200 calories, FAT 21 g, PROTEIN 1 g, CARB 4 g, FIBER 2 g, CHOL 0 mg, IRON 1 mg, SODIUM 939 mg, CALC 27 mg

Arugula, Bell Pepper, and Pepperoni Salad

We learned this wonderful Italian salad from a favorite restaurant in Carroll Gardens, Brooklyn. It combines spicy arugula, sweet bell pepper, and salty pepperoni for a satisfying foil to any grilled meat.

Preparation time: 15 minutes

MAKES 2 SERVINGS

2 tablespoons red wine vinegar

3 tablespoons extra-virgin olive oil

1 garlic clove, finely chopped

½ red bell pepper, seeded and coarsely chopped

½ yellow bell pepper, seeded and coarsely chopped

1 bunch arugula, stems removed

3 ounces pepperoni, thinly sliced

2 tablespoon drained capers

Salt and freshly milled pepper to taste

In medium bowl, combine the red wine vinegar, olive oil, and chopped garlic. Toss in the bell peppers, arugula, pepperoni, and capers. Toss thoroughly. Taste and add salt and pepper as needed. Chill until just before serving.

Nutritional Analysis: 424 calories, FAT 40 g, PROTEIN 10 g, CARB 8 g, FIBER 2 g, CHOL 34 mg, IRON 1 mg, SODIUM 1,767 mg, CALC 23 mg

Beet, Fennel, and Walnut Chutney

Red beets, crunchy fennel, and walnuts flavored with basil and tarragon—what a combo. If you've sworn off beets as a high-carb food, welcome them back to your diet, judiciously.

Preparation time: 15 minutes

MAKES 2 SERVINGS

2 tablespoons extra-virgin olive oil

2 tablespoon fresh lemon juice

½ teaspoon sugar

1 tablespoon chopped fresh basil

1 tablespoon fresh tarragon leaves

Half a 14-ounce can beets, drained and chopped

1 fennel bulb, cored and chopped

¼ cup walnuts, toasted

Salt and freshly milled pepper to taste

In a medium bowl, combine the olive oil, lemon juice, sugar, basil, and tarragon. Add the beets, fennel, and walnuts. Toss thoroughly. Taste and add salt and pepper as needed. Chill until just before serving.

Nutritional Analysis: 150 calories, FAT 12 g, PROTEIN 2 g, CARB 11 g, FIBER 3 g, CHOL 0 mg, IRON 2 mg, SODIUM 418 mg, CALC 49 mg

Wilted Escarole and Bacon Slaw

The bitter flavor of escarole juxtaposed with the salty flavor of bacon, all complemented by cognac and vinegar, lifts any menu to delicious heights.

MAKES 2 SERVINGS

Preparation time: 15 minutes

Cooking time: 10 minutes

1 tablespoon extra-virgin olive oil

3 ounces bacon, chopped

1 garlic clove, chopped

1 tablespoon red wine vinegar

1 tablespoon cognac

8 ounces escarole, washed and shredded

Salt and freshly milled pepper to taste

In a medium skillet, combine the olive oil and bacon and cook over medium-low heat for 5 to 6 minutes. Add the garlic and cook for 1 minute. Add the vinegar and cognac, stir, then add the shredded escarole and cook for 1 more minute, tossing thoroughly. The escarole will wilt just a bit. Taste and add salt and pepper as needed. Serve at once.

Nutritional Analysis: 183 calories, FAT 14 g, PROTEIN 6 g, CARB 5 g, FIBER 4 g, CHOL 12 mg, IRON 1 mg, SODIUM 830 mg, CALC 66 mg

Ginger Jicama Slaw

The bright flavors of ginger and jicama make a meal feel exotic. Pair this salad with pork, beef, chicken, or fish. Hell, just eat it plain. You will love it.

Preparation time: 15 minutes

MAKES 2 SERVINGS

2 tablespoons cider vinegar

2 tablespoons extra-virgin olive oil

1 tablespoon Dijon mustard

1 tablespoon ketchup

½ packet sugar substitute (optional)

1 garlic clove, finely chopped

1 cup shredded cabbage

½ cup julienned jicama

¼ cup julienned carrot

1 tablespoon chopped fresh ginger

¼ cup chopped fresh cilantro

Salt and freshly milled pepper to taste

In a medium bowl, combine the vinegar, olive oil, mustard, ketchup, sugar substitute, and garlic. Mix thoroughly. Toss in the cabbage, jicama, carrot, ginger, and cilantro and mix well. Taste and add salt and pepper as needed.

Nutritional Analysis: 182 calories, FAT 15 g, PROTEIN 2 g, CARB 12 g, FIBER 3 g, CHOL 0 mg, IRON 1 mg, SODIUM 1 mg, CALC 45 mg

Green Beans and Jicama Salad

The crunch of jicama makes this an unusually satisfying bean salad; pack it on your next picnic.

MAKES 2 SERVINGS

Preparation time: 10 minutes

Cooking time: 5 minutes

4 ounces green beans, trimmed

2 tablespoons red wine vinegar

1 teaspoon ground cumin

3 tablespoons fresh lime juice

2 tablespoons extra-virgin olive oil

2 tablespoons chopped fresh cilantro

½ medium tomato, chopped

4 ounces jicama, peeled and cut in thin
  julienne strips

Bring water to a boil in a medium sauce pan. Boil the green beans for about 5 minutes, just until they are bright green and a little softened. Drain well. Meanwhile, in a medium bowl, combine the vinegar, cumin, lime juice, and olive oil. Toss in the cilantro, tomato, jicama, and the green beans.

Nutritional Analysis: 153 calories, FAT 14 g, PROTEIN 1 g, CARB 7 g, FIBER 2 g, CHOL 0 mg, IRON 1 mg, SODIUM 6 mg, CALC 21 mg

Lemongrass Hot and Spicy Cabbage Slaw

The flavors of lemongrass and hot pepper will really get your juices flowing. This mouthwatering slaw goes with beef, pork, chicken, or fish.

MAKES 2 SERVINGS

Preparation time: 10 minutes
Marinating time: 10 minutes

3 tablespoons rice wine vinegar

2 tablespoons vegetable oil

1 garlic clove

¼ teaspoon cayenne

½ teaspoon sugar

1 tablespoon ketchup

1 tablespoon chopped fresh ginger

1 teaspoon salt

3 lemongrass stalks, white bottom portions
    only

8 ounces Chinese cabbage, thinly sliced

½ medium carrot, peeled and shredded

1 teaspoon freshly milled black pepper

In a medium bowl, combine the vinegar, oil, garlic, cayenne, sugar, ketchup, ginger, salt, and lemongrass. Let it stand for 10 minutes. Toss in the cabbage and carrot. Taste and add salt and black pepper as needed. Remove the lemongrass just before serving.

Nutritional Analysis: 172 calories, FAT 14 g, PROTEIN 2 g, CARB 10 g, FIBER 5 g,
CHOL 0 mg, IRON 1 mg, SODIUM 1,271 mg, CALC 103 mg

Red Cabbage, Blue Cheese, and Apple Slaw

Walnut oil is an earthy alternative to olive oil. Its distinct yet subtle flavor really adds to this complex slaw. Serve it with lamb, pork, or chicken.

MAKES 2 SERVINGS

Preparation time: 15 minutes

2 tablespoons red wine vinegar

3 tablespoons walnut oil

2 teaspoons Dijon mustard

8 ounces cabbage, shredded

½ unpeeled green apple, cored and grated

Salt and freshly milled pepper to taste

2½ ounces blue cheese, crumbled

In a medium bowl, combine the vinegar, walnut oil, and mustard; mix well. Toss in the cabbage, apple, and salt and pepper. Taste and adjust seasoning. Add the blue cheese and toss again.

Nutritional Analysis: 360 calories, FAT 31 g, PROTEIN 10 g, CARB 14 g, FIBER 3 g,
CHOL 27 mg, IRON 1 mg, SODIUM 1,222 mg, CALC 251 mg

Roasted Red Pepper and Feta Salsa

Roasted red pepper, thyme, and feta cheese combine to make a fresh, rich-tasting salad to serve with any grilled lamb. The robust olives marry nicely with the earthy feta cheese.

Preparation time: 15 minutes

MAKES 2 SERVINGS

1 tablespoon red wine vinegar

2 tablespoons fresh lemon juice

2 tablespoons finely chopped fresh thyme

¼ small red onion, finely chopped

1 garlic clove, finely chopped

2 tablespoons extra-virgin olive oil

⅓ cup drained Greek olives

2 roasted red bell peppers, seeded and chopped (page 22)

6 ounces feta cheese, crumbled

Salt and freshly milled black pepper to taste

In a medium bowl, combine the vinegar, lemon juice, thyme, red onion, garlic, and olive oil. Toss in the olives, peppers, and feta cheese. Taste and add salt and pepper as needed; the feta will be quite salty.

Nutritional Analysis: 371 calories, FAT 32 g, PROTEIN 13 g, CARB 9 g, FIBER 1 g, CHOL 76 mg, IRON 1 mg, SODIUM 1,542 mg, CALC 457 mg

Warm Roasted Asparagus and Pimiento Salad

Warm asparagus tossed in the vinaigrette and garnished with the salty pimientos leaves you feeling totally satisfied. Serve with grilled chicken or fish or beef.

MAKES 2 SERVINGS

Preparation time: 15 minutes

Roasting time: 10 minutes

12 ounces asparagus

3 tablespoons extra-virgin olive oil

1 garlic clove, chopped

2 tablespoons white wine vinegar

¼ teaspoon Dijon mustard

1 tablespoon finely chopped fresh flat-leaf parsley

3 tablespoons chopped pimientos

2 tablespoons fresh lemon juice

Salt and freshly milled black pepper to taste

Preheat the oven to 400° F. Wash the asparagus. Hold each piece in your fingers and snap off the bottom where it breaks naturally. Slice each spear diagonally into 1-inch pieces. Toss the asparagus with 2 tablespoons of the olive oil and the chopped garlic. Arrange the chopped spears in the bottom of a well-greased 14-inch glass baking dish. Roast for 10 minutes.

Meanwhile, in a medium bowl, mix together the vinegar, mustard, parsley, pimientos, lemon juice, and remaining olive oil. Taste and add salt and pepper as needed.

Add the roasted asparagus pieces to the dressing and toss thoroughly. Serve warm or at room temperature.

Nutritional Analysis: 241 calories, FAT 21 g, PROTEIN 4 g, CARB 11 g, FIBER 4 g, CHOL 0 mg, IRON 2 mg, SODIUM 606 mg, CALC 47 mg

Warm Kale and Red Onion Salad

Kale has a wonderful bitter flavor that is a great foil for a subtle dish such as chicken, but it also stands up to a more gamy main course such as lamb.

Preparation time: 15 minutes

Cooking time: 10 minutes

MAKES 2 SERVINGS

3 tablespoons extra-virgin olive oil

1 medium shallot, minced

1 tablespoon red wine vinegar

8 ounces kale, washed and dried

1 medium green bell pepper, chopped

¼ medium red onion, chopped

Salt and freshly milled pepper to taste

2 tablespoons drained capers

In a medium saucepan, heat 2 tablespoons of the olive oil over medium heat. Stir in the shallots and sauté for 1 minute. Stir in the vinegar and kale and cook for 1 more minute, just until the kale wilts. Divide the kale between two plates. In the same pan heat remaining tablespoon of olive oil. Stir in the pepper, onion, and salt and pepper. Cook over medium-high heat for about 5 minutes, stirring occasionally. Top the kale with the bell peppers and onion and garnish with the capers. Serve at once.

Nutritional Analysis: 243 calories, FAT 22 g, PROTEIN 4 g, CARB 12 g, FIBER 4 g, CHOL 0 mg, IRON 2 mg, SODIUM 927 mg, CALC 102 mg

Watercress Endive and Goat Cheese Salad

The earthy flavor of goat cheese, combined with the spicy watercress and the bitter endive, is a great foil for the sweetened vinaigrette. The sweetness is delicious when matched to any grilled meats.

Preparation time: 15 minutes

MAKES 2 SERVINGS

2 tablespoons raspberry vinegar

½ teaspoon Dijon mustard

¼ packet sugar substitute (optional)

2 tablespoons extra-virgin olive oil

1 tablespoon black olives

1 head Belgian endive, leaves separated

1 bunch watercress, stems removed

2 ounces goat cheese, crumbled

Salt and freshly milled pepper to taste

In a medium bowl, mix together the vinegar, mustard, sugar substitute if using, and olive oil. Toss in the olives, endive, watercress, and goat cheese. Taste and add salt and pepper as needed.

Nutritional Analysis: 27 calories, FAT 1 g, PROTEIN 2 g, CARB 3 g, FIBER 1 g,
CHOL 2 mg, IRON 1 mg, SODIUM 650 mg, CALC 38 mg

VEGETABLE PURÉES: ELEVEN REASONS NOT TO EAT MASHED POTATOES

Don't write vegetable purées off as baby food. They are deliciously sophisticated, combining interesting flavors and beautiful colors into a wonderful comfort food texture. You can pair them with any grilled meat with a dry rub. Most of the recipes serve four (they store and reheat well) and contain fewer than 15 grams of carbohydrates per serving. Give them a try.

Avocado Purée

This silky smooth, very rich purée adds bright color and a calming effect to the main course. Try it with a particularly spicy main course for a true yin and yang effect. Avocado discolors when exposed to air, so don't make this too far ahead of time.

Preparation time: 10 minutes

MAKES 2 SERVINGS

1 medium avocado
2 tablespoons sour cream
2 tablespoons fresh lemon juice
Salt and freshly milled black pepper to taste

Combine all the ingredients in a food processor or blender. Process until smooth. Serve immediately.

Nutritional Analysis: 198 calories, FAT 18 g, PROTEIN 3 g, CARB 10 g, FIBER 5 g, CHOL 6 mg, IRON 1 mg, SODIUM 599 mg, CALC 31 mg

Beet and Coriander Purée

Heighten the flavor of beets with the exotic flavor of coriander. Garnish with a little fresh cilantro for a beautiful, jewel-toned, purple and green dish. You could also substitute 2 tablespoons of horseradish for the coriander for a different flavor.

Preparation time: 10 minutes

Cooking time: 10 minutes

MAKES 4 SERVINGS

2 tablespoons unsalted butter

½ medium onion, finely chopped

One 14-ounce can beets, drained

1 tablespoon cider vinegar

½ teaspoon sugar

1 teaspoon ground coriander

Cilantro for garnish

In a medium skillet, over medium heat, melt the butter and sauté the onions for about 3 minutes, or until they are translucent. Meanwhile, in a food processor or blender, mix the beets, vinegar, sugar, and coriander. Add the purée to the pan and simmer on low for another 7 minutes. Garnish with cilantro and serve.

Nutritional Analysis: 91 calories, FAT 6 g, PROTEIN 1 g, CARB 10 g, FIBER 2 g, CHOL 15 mg, IRON 2 mg, SODIUM 243 mg, CALC 23 mg

Broccoli and Spinach with Ricotta Cheese

This is a great way to eat your broccoli and spinach and get a little protein boost to boot. Sorry, George Bush, this broccoli is great. Get creative and try different spices, such as cumin, coriander or mint.

MAKES 4 SERVINGS

Preparation time: 10 minutes
Cooking time: 7 minutes

½ medium onion, chopped

8 ounces broccoli florets plus peeled and
    chopped stems

10 ounces spinach, washed thoroughly and
    stems removed

½ cup ricotta cheese

2 garlic cloves

2 tablespoons fresh lemon juice

2 tablespoons unsalted butter

½ teaspoon ground nutmeg

Salt and freshly milled black pepper to taste

Bring 3 quarts of water to a boil. Add the onion and broccoli and cook for 5 minutes or until fork tender. Add the spinach and cook for 2 minutes longer. Drain the vegetables and transfer to the bowl of a food processor or blender. Add the ricotta cheese, garlic, lemon juice, butter, nutmeg, and salt and freshly milled black pepper. Pulse until thoroughly blended. Taste and adjust the seasoning. Serve hot.

Nutritional Analysis: 136 calories, FAT 9 g, PROTEIN 8 g, CARB 10 g, FIBER 4 g,
CHOL 24 mg, IRON 3 mg, SODIUM 451 mg, CALC 192 mg

Cauliflower Purée

Even plain, the flavor of this purée is delicious. You can get fancy with it, however. Blend in a cup of arugula, add a tablespoon of fresh ginger or horseradish. Cauliflower is practically carb-free and should replace potatoes in you diet permanently.

Preparation time: 10 minutes

Cooking time: 10 minutes

MAKES 4 SERVINGS

12 ounces cauliflower florets and peeled stems

2 tablespoons unsalted butter

¼ cup heavy cream

¼ cup grated Parmesan cheese

Salt and freshly milled black pepper to taste

Over high heat, bring 4 quarts of water to boil. Add the cauliflower and cook for 10 minutes, or until fork-tender. Drain and transfer to the bowl of a food processor or blender. Add the butter, cream, Parmesan, and salt and pepper. Purée, then taste and adjust the seasonings.

Nutritional Analysis: 152 calories, FAT 13 g, PROTEIN 5 g, CARB 5 g, FIBER 2 g, CHOL 40 mg, IRON 1 mg, SODIUM 488 mg, CALC 118 mg

Carrots and Yellow Summer Squash

The beautiful yellow color of this delicious accompaniment will remind you of the sun. Mother Nature? God made the flavors good, we just put them together!

MAKES 4 SERVINGS

Preparation time: 10 minutes

Cooking time: 12 minutes

2 tablespoons olive oil

1 shallot, minced

2 tablespoons ground fresh ginger

12 ounces yellow crookneck squash, cut in chunks

1 medium carrot, peeled and sliced

1 tablespoon unsalted butter

Salt and freshly milled black pepper to taste

In a large skillet, combine the olive oil, shallot, and ginger and sauté over medium-high heat for about 2 minutes. Add the summer squash and carrot and stir thoroughly. Cover and simmer for 15 minutes, stirring occasionally. Drain off any excess liquid and transfer to the bowl of a food processor or blender. Purée until smooth. Add the butter and salt and pepper and purée again. Taste and adjust the seasonings.

Nutritional Analysis: 119 calories, FAT 3 g, PROTEIN 1 g, CARB 7 g, FIBER 2 g, CHOL 8 mg, IRON 1 mg, SODIUM 325 mg, CALC 27 mg

Celeriac Purée

Celeriac has a delicious salty celery-like flavor with a velvety texture. Try this purée for something different. Don't be shy with the pepper!

MAKES 4 SERVINGS

Preparation time: 10 minutes

Cooking time: 7 minutes

8 ounces celeriac, peeled and chopped into
  2-inch chunks

2 tablespoons unsalted butter

¼ cup heavy cream

2 tablespoons chopped fresh ginger

Salt and freshly milled black pepper to taste

Bring 4 quarts of water to a boil over high heat. Add the celeriac and cook for 7 minutes, or until fork-tender. Drain and transfer to the bowl of a food processor or blender. Add the butter, cream, ginger, and salt and pepper and purée until smooth. Taste and adjust the seasonings.

Nutritional Analysis: 252 calories, FAT 22 g, PROTEIN 3 g, CARB 13 g, FIBER 2 g, CHOL 70 mg, IRON 2 mg, SODIUM 806 mg, CALC 76 mg

Eggplant and Red Pepper Purée

Eggplants are enjoyed all over the world, and their flavor is extremely versatile. Try them with ginger, curry, or sharp olives; you can't go wrong. This recipe renders a copper-colored purée that is beautiful next to anything. What a wonderful way to enjoy eggplant.

Preparation time: 10 minutes
Cooking time: 20 minutes

MAKES 4 SERVINGS

1 medium eggplant, peeled and cubed

½ medium onion, chopped

2 tablespoons olive oil

¾ cup roasted red bell peppers, seeded
   (page 22)

2 tablespoons unsalted butter

Salt and freshly milled black pepper to taste

Preheat the broiler. In a small bowl, toss the eggplant cubes and onion thoroughly in the olive oil. Place them on a baking sheet 4 to 6 inches from the broiler and cook, stirring the onion and eggplant chunks every few minutes, for 20 minutes, or until the eggplant is fork-tender. Transfer to the bowl of a food processor or blender and add the red peppers, butter, and salt and pepper. Purée until smooth, then taste and adjust the seasonings.

Nutritional Analysis: 140 calories, FAT 13 g, PROTEIN .1 g, CARB 6 g, FIBER 2 g,
CHOL 15 mg, IRON 0 mg, SODIUM 369 mg, CALC 12 mg

Fennel Purée

This white purée ends up with a hint of licorice. Try blending it with other members of the lily family such as leeks, garlic, and shallots. Great with fish or other subtle-flavored main courses. Fennel is a Mediterranean plant with a mild licorice flavor. The feathery greenery is used as an herb, the bulb as a vegetable, and the seeds as a spice. Fennel seeds are milder and sweeter than anise seeds, which may be used as a substitute.

Preparation time: 10 minutes
Cooking time: 7 minutes

MAKES 4 SERVINGS

1 pound fennel bulb, cored and chopped
   into chunks

½ medium onion, cut in chunks

2 tablespoons unsalted butter

Salt and freshly milled black pepper
   to taste

Over high heat, bring 4 quarts of water to a boil. Add the fennel and onion and cook for 10 minutes, or until fork-tender. Drain and transfer to the bowl of a food processor or blender. Add the butter and a generous amount of salt and pepper and purée until smooth. Taste and adjust the seasonings.

Nutritional Analysis: 93 calories, FAT 6 g, PROTEIN 2 g, CARB 10 g, FIBER 4 g, CHOL 15 mg, IRON 1 mg, SODIUM 400 mg, CALC 63 mg

Spinach, Mint, and Ricotta Purée

This minty, garlicky delight is a compelling complement to beef, lamb, or fish. It is so high in protein that it could almost be a meal. Try substituting cilantro or basil for the mint, for a change.

Preparation time: 10 minutes
Cooking time: 5 minutes

MAKES 4 SERVINGS

2 tablespoons olive oil

1 garlic clove, chopped

15 ounces spinach leaves, washed thoroughly, and stems removed

3 tablespoons water

1½ cups mint leaves

½ cup ricotta cheese

1 tablespoon fresh lemon juice

1 tablespoon heavy cream

Salt and freshly milled black pepper to taste

Over medium-high heat, heat the olive oil in a skillet for 1 minute. Add the garlic, spinach, and water and cook for 3 to 4 minutes, just until the spinach is wilted. Drain and transfer to the bowl of a food processor or blender. Add the mint, ricotta cheese, lemon juice, heavy cream, and salt and pepper and purée. Taste and adjust the seasonings.

Nutritional Analysis: 296 calories, FAT 22 g, PROTEIN 14 g, CARB 13 g, FIBER 5 g, CHOL 30 mg, IRON 6 mg, SODIUM 830 mg, CALC 418 mg

Zucchini and Yellow Squash Purée

Even people who aren't zucchini fans will find this light squash purée very comforting. Better still, it's delicious warm or cold. Be sure to add a lot of pepper.

MAKES 4 SERVINGS

Preparation time: 10 minutes

Cooking time: 7 minutes

2 tablespoons olive oil

½ onion, thinly sliced

8 ounces yellow summer squash, thinly sliced

8 ounces small zucchini, thinly sliced

Salt to taste

3 tablespoons water

¼ cup heavy cream

Freshly milled black pepper to taste

Over medium-high heat, heat the olive oil in a skillet. Add the onion and cook for 5 minutes, until the onion is translucent. Add the squash and zucchini with a little salt. Sauté until the vegetables start to give up their liquid. Add the water, cover, and cook for 10 minutes, or until fork-tender. Drain the vegetables and transfer to the bowl of a food processor or blender. Add the cream and pepper and process until smooth. Taste and adjust the seasonings.

Nutritional Analysis: 282 calories, FAT 26 g, PROTEIN 3 g, CARB 13 g, FIBER 3.5 g, CHOL 41 mg, IRON 1 mg, SODIUM 596 mg, CALC 80 mg

Zucchini, Eggplant, and Cilantro Purée

This Indian-influenced dish will win your heart and make you long for the subcontinent.

MAKES 4 SERVINGS

Preparation time: 10 minutes

Cooking time: 7 minutes

2 tablespoons olive oil

8 ounces zucchini, cubed

8 ounces eggplant, cubed

1 teaspoon chili powder

¼ cup chopped fresh cilantro

3 tablespoons water

Salt and freshly milled black pepper to taste

Preheat the broiler. On a broiler pan, toss the zucchini and eggplant cubes thoroughly in the olive oil. Place 4 to 6 inches from the broiler and cook, stirring every few minutes, for 15 to 20 minutes or until the eggplant is fork tender. Transfer to the bowl of a food processor or blender and add the chili powder and cilantro, and salt and pepper. Process to make a smooth purée. Taste and adjust seasonings.

Nutritional Analysis: 188 calories, FAT 14 g, PROTEIN 3 g, CARB 15 g, FIBER 5 g, CHOL 0 mg, IRON 1 mg, SODIUM 603 mg, CALC .39 mg

DESSERTS: NO-GUILT PLEASURES

You know how it is. When you gotta have it,
you gotta have it. We don't eat dessert every day. But from time to time, we
just have to have a really drop-dead dessert to make us feel like real people.

We worked hard to convert some of our favorites for you to try. We offer
them with a couple of caveats and also some breakthrough news about what
will work and what won't.

In the first place, some of these desserts make more than two servings.
That's okay. You can keep the leftovers in the refrigerator for a day or two.
Some of them take a tad more time than our main dishes do. That's okay, too.
Hey, it's dessert. You're worth it.

But our real breakthrough has to do with flavor. In trying many so-called
low-carb desserts that relied on artificial sweeteners, we discovered the judi-

cious addition of a tablespoon of sugar to a recipe sometimes lifted the flavor in a way artificial sweeteners simply could not. And the havoc that simple spoonful of sugar wrecked on the total nutritional readout was minimal.

If we are doctrinaire about anything in our work, it's flavor. We simply don't put recipes in our books that don't get a pass from our various taste panel members: Katherine, Gordon, Lily, Noel, Linda, Joe, and sometimes the dogs. If they all lick their chops, we figure it goes in. All of these recipes passed. So don't eliminate dessert from your high-protein regimen.

Meringue Torte with Lemon Filling and Strawberries

Who needs pie crust? Make a meringue crust, then fill it with our fantastic lemon filling. Top it off with fresh strawberries. Now that's dessert.

MAKES 6 SERVINGS

Preparation time: 20 minutes

Cooking time: 20 minutes

Cooling time: 20 minutes

MERINGUE SHELL

3 large egg whites

¼ teaspoon cream of tartar

¼ teaspoon kosher salt

10 packets aspartame sweetener

FILLING

2¼ cups water

Grated zest of 1 lemon plus ⅔ cup fresh lemon juice

½ teaspoon kosher salt

30 packets aspartame sweetener

⅓ cup plus 2 tablespoons cornstarch

2 large eggs

2 large egg whites

2 tablespoons unsalted butter

Preheat the oven to 325°F. Make the meringe shell: Beat the 3 egg whites in a medium bowl until foamy. Add the cream of tartar, salt, and sweetener and beat to stiff peaks. Line a baking sheet with parchment paper and pour the meringue onto the paper. Use a rubber spatula to form an indented circle about 9 inches in diameter. Alternatively, form into 6 individual circles. Bake until brown, 15 to 20 minutes for a large meringue, 10 to 15 minutes for individual meringues. Cool on a wire rack.

Meanwhile, make the filling: Mix the water, lemon zest and juice, salt, sweetener, and cornstarch in a medium saucepan. Bring to a boil over medium-high heat, stirring constantly. Boil and stir for 1 minute, then remove from the heat.

Beat two eggs and two egg whites in a small bowl. Stir in about half of the hot cornstarch mixture, then stir this egg mixture back into the cornstarch mixture remaining in the pan. Cook and stir over low heat for 1 minute. Remove from the heat and swirl in the butter. Pour the mixture into the cooked and cooled meringue shell. Top with the sliced strawberries, and serve at once.

Nutritional Analysis: 102 calories, FAT 4 g, PROTEIN 4 g, CARB 12 g, FIBER 1 g, CHOL 61 mg, IRON 0 mg, SODIUM 222 mg, CALC 16 mg

Chocolate Amaretto Fondue with Fresh Berries

What could be more satisfying than dipping perfectly ripe, sweet berries into hot, sensuous chocolate? Choose strawberries, blackberries, marionberries, or raspberries.

Refrigerate the fondue you don't eat at one meal, then zap it in the microwave a moment to warm it before using again.

MAKES 4 SERVINGS

Preparation time: 5 minutes
Cooking time: 5 minutes

3 ounces unsweetened baking chocolate

1 cup heavy cream

24 packets aspartame sweetener

1 tablespoon sugar

1 teaspoon amaretto

1 teaspoon vanilla extract

Berries of your choice, about ½ cup per serving

Break the chocolate into small pieces and place in a 2-cup glass measure with the cream. Heat in the microwave on high (100 percent power), until the chocolate is melted, about 2 minutes (or heat in a double-broiler over low heat, whisking constantly). Whisk until the mixture is shiny.

Add the sweetener, sugar, amaretto, and vanilla, whisking until the mixture is smooth.

Transfer the mixture to a fondue pot or a serving bowl. Serve with berries for dipping.

Nutritional Analysis: 350 calories, FAT 34 g, PROTEIN 4 g, CARB. 15 g, FIBER 5 g, CHOL 82 mg, IRON 2 mg, SODIUM 26 mg, CALC 61 mg

Individual Flans with a Raspberry Coulis

Unmold these sensuous little flans onto dessert plates and drizzle raspberry coulis atop. Finish with a spoonful of fresh raspberries. Feel deprived now?

MAKES 6 SERVINGS

Preparation time: 5 minutes
Cooking time: 20 minutes
Chilling time: 2 hours

1 cup milk

1 cup half-and-half

2 large eggs

2 large egg yolks

6 packets aspartame sweetener

¼ teaspoon kosher salt

1 teaspoon vanilla extract

1 cup fresh raspberries plus additional berries for garnish

Mint sprigs for garnish (optional)

Place a roasting pan filled with 1 inch of water on a rack in the lower third of the oven. Preheat the oven to 325°F. Butter six ½-inch ramekins. Heat the milk and half-and-half in the microwave on high (100 percent power) for 2 minutes or on the stovetop in a medium saucepan until warm.

Meanwhile, beat the eggs and egg yolks in a medium bowl until foamy. Gradually whisk the hot milk mixture into the eggs. Stir in the sweetener, salt, and vanilla. Pour the mixture into the prepared ramekins. Cover each dish with aluminum foil. Place in the water-filled saucepans and bake until the custards are set, about 30 minutes. To check, insert a knife into the center of the custard; if it comes out clean, it's done.

Remove the dishes from the roasting pan and cool to room temperature on a wire rack, then refrigerate until chilled, about 2 hours.

To make the coulis, simply purée the raspberries in the food processor. Add sweetener to taste (usually not needed with sweet, fully ripe berries). Transfer to a pitcher and refrigerate.

To serve, run a spoon around the edge of each custard and turn it out onto a dessert plate. Drizzle coulis over the top of the custard and finish with a few fresh raspberries and a sprig of mint, if using.

Nutritional Analysis: 135 calories, FAT 9 g, PROTEIN 6 g, CARB 6 g, FIBER 1 g, CHOL 167 mg, IRON 1 mg, SODIUM 160 mg, CALC 109 mg

Nearly Flourless Chocolate Cake with Whipped Cream and Raspberries

Who knew this restaurant classic would be so easy to convert? Save this splurge for a day when you're willing to give up half your daily carbohydrate allowance for one fine piece of cake. We all have such days.

Preparation time: 10 minutes
Baking time: 20 minutes
Chilling time: 1 hour

MAKES 12 SERVINGS

Cocoa for dusting the pan

6 tablespoons unsalted butter

4 ounces unsweetened chocolate

⅓ cup half-and-half

⅓ cup raspberry all-fruit preserves

1 teaspoon instant espresso powder

1 tablespoon sugar

3 large eggs, separated

1 teaspoon vanilla extract

22 packets aspartame sweetener

⅛ teaspoon cream of tartar

¼ cup all-purpose flour

⅛ teaspoon salt

1 cup heavy cream

½ cup raspberries for garnish (optional)

Preheat the oven to 350°F. Line a 9-inch cake pan with a piece of buttered parchment paper, buttered side down. Butter the top of the paper and dust with cocoa, knocking out the excess. Set it aside.

Combine the butter, chocolate, half-and-half, raspberry preserves, and espresso powder in a microwave-safe dish. Heat in the microwave on high (100 percent power) until the chocolate is melted, 2 to 3 minutes. Alternatively, use a double boiler on low heat on the stovetop. Remove and let cool.

Whisk in the sugar, egg yolks, and vanilla. Add the aspartame, whisking until smooth.

In another bowl, beat the egg whites until foamy, then add the cream of tartar and beat to stiff peaks. Fold the chocolate mixture (it should be cool to the touch) into the egg whites, then fold in the combined flour and salt, taking care not to overmix. Pour into the prepared pan. Bake just until the cake is firm when lightly touched, 18 to 20 minutes, or until a toothpick inserted in the center comes out clean. Take care not to overbake. Place the cake on a rack and run a knife around the edge to loosen it and remove from the pan. Cool completely on a cake rack, then refrigerate until chilled, 1 to 2 hours.

To serve, whip the cream to soft peaks. Cut the cake in small wedges and serve each one with a dollop of whipped cream and some raspberries.

Nutritional Analysis: 222 calories, FAT 20 g, PROTEIN 3 g, CARB 10 g, FIBER 2 g, CHOL 99 mg, IRON 1 mg, SODIUM 103 mg, CALC 450 mg

Flan Almendra

Flan is a wonderful palate cleanser. The silken texture will contribute a happy ending to any meal.

MAKES 4 SERVINGS

Preparation time: 5 minutes

Cooking time: 20 minutes

1¼ cups whole milk

4 large eggs

3 packets aspartame sweetener, or to taste

1 tablespoon sugar

1 teaspoon vanilla extract

1 teaspoon almond extract (optional)

¼ cup slivered almonds

½ cup berries of your choice for garnish (optional)

Place a roasting pan filled with 1 inch of water in the oven and preheat to 325°F. Butter 4 ramekins or glass custard cups.

Warm the milk in a 1-quart, microwave-safe bowl for 2 minutes on high (100 percent power). Alternatively, heat on the stovetop in a medium saucepan to just under a boil.

Meanwhile, in another bowl, whisk together the eggs, sweetener, sugar, vanilla, and almond extract, if using. Pour the hot milk into the egg mixture and stir to blend.

Toast the almonds by heating them in a small dry skillet just until they begin to brown, about 1 minute. Divide the almonds among the 4 ramekins, then fill with the custard. Cover with aluminum foil. Place the ramekins in the water bath. Bake until the custards are set, about 20 minutes. To test, insert a knife in the middle; it should come out clean.

Serve at room temperature or chilled. To serve, run a knife around the edge of the ramekin, then turn out the flan onto a dessert plate. If you wish, add ½ cup of berries of your choice.

Nutritional Analysis: 193 calories, FAT 12 g, PROTEIN 11 g, CARB 9 g, FIBER 1 g, CHOL 223 mg, IRON 1 mg, SODIUM 101 mg, CALC 137 mg

Spiced Strawberries

Strawberries are an elegant ending. Spice them up with a little vinegar and black pepper and you won't regret it.

MAKES 4 SERVINGS

Preparation time: 5 minutes

Chilling time: 15 minutes

2 cups halved strawberries

1 tablespoon sugar

2 teaspoon sherry vinegar

$\frac{1}{4}$ teaspoon finely milled black pepper

Toss the berries with the sugar, vinegar, and pepper in a medium bowl. Cover and chill for at least 15 minutes. Serve in footed dessert dishes.

Nutritional Analysis: 34 calories, FAT .2 g, PROTEIN .5 g, CARB 8 g, FIBER 2 g, CHOL 0 mg, IRON .3 mg, SODIUM 1 mg, CALC 11 mg

Blackberry Fool

Eat this English dessert once, and you'll see why it's called a "fool." You'll be a fool for it yourself. Can't buy crème fraîche? Start a day ahead and whip up your own. It's easy.

MAKES 2 SERVINGS

Preparation time: 10 minutes

Chilling time: 30 minutes

1 cup crème fraîche, or 1 tablespoon sour cream plus 1 cup heavy cream

1 cup blackberries

1 tablespoon sugar

1 packet aspartame sweetener, or to taste

$\frac{1}{8}$ teaspoon crème de cassis

If you can't buy crème fraîche, simply blend the sour cream and heavy cream. Cover and let it stand at room temperature 6 to 8 hours. Refrigerate, covered, 24 hours before using.

Set aside 6 gorgeous blackberries. Combine the remaining berries with sugar, sweetener, crème de cassis, and crème fraîche. Gently mix, then spoon into footed dessert dishes. Cover and chill until serving time. Garnish with the reserved berries.

Nutritional Analysis: 244 calories, FAT 23 g, PROTEIN 2 g, CARB 10 g, FIBER 2 g, CHOL 83 mg, IRON 0 mg, CALC 54 mg

Zabaglione

Come home to Italy for a sweet finish.

MAKES 4 SERVINGS

Preparation time: 10 minutes

Cooking time: 15 minutes

6 large egg yolks

2 packets aspartame sweetener

¼ cup Marsala

1 tablespoon grated orange zest

3 tablespoons Grand Marnier

1 cup heavy cream, whipped to soft peaks

Beat the egg yolks and sweetener in the top of a double boiler, set over simmering water, until pale yellow and thick, 3 to 5 minutes. Add the Marsala and orange zest and continue cooking, whisking vigorously, until the mixture thickens enough to coat the back of a spoon. Remove from the heat and stir in the Grand Marnier.

Divide among four dessert dishes. Serve warm or chilled. Top each serving with ¼ cup of whipped cream. Alternatively, chill the zabaglione and fold in the whipped cream, then divide among the dessert dishes.

Nutritional Analysis: 343 calories, FAT 30 g, PROTEIN 6 g, CARB 4 g, FIBER .1 g, CHOL 400 mg, IRON 1 mg, SODIUM 35 mg, CALC 76 mg

Raspberries and Cream

Two hits of tart raspberries make this especially flavorful.

MAKES 2 SERVINGS

Preparation time: 10 minutes

Chilling time: 30 minutes

½ cup heavy cream

¼ teaspoon vanilla extract

1 tablespoon sugar

½ packet aspartame sweetener

1 pint fresh raspberries

Whip the cream with the vanilla, sugar, and aspartame until it forms soft peaks. Crush half the raspberries with a spoon and fold into the cream. Divide the remaining berries among four dessert bowls and top with the raspberry cream. Cover and refrigerate until serving time.

Nutritional Analysis: 145 calories, FAT 11 g, PROTEIN 1 g, CARB 11 g, FIBER 4 g, CHOL 41 g, IRON .3 g, SODIUM 11 g, CALC .33 mg

Strawberries and Melon Balls in Bourbon

Nothing like a little inebriation to perk up all those berries and melon balls.

MAKES 2 SERVINGS

Preparation time: 20 minutes

Chilling time: 20 minutes

½ cup melon balls (cantaloupe, Crenshaw, or
  a mixture)
½ cup halved strawberries
1 tablespoon bourbon

1 tablespoon sugar
½ packet aspartame sweetener, or to taste
Sprigs of fresh mint for garnish

Combine the melon balls and strawberries in a glass dish. Toss with the bourbon, sugar, and aspartame. Cover and refrigerate until serving time. Spoon the fruit into dessert dishes and decorate with mint leaves.

Nutritional Analysis: 68 calories, FAT .2 g, PROTEIN .6 g, CARB 13 g, FIBER 2.2 g,
CHOL 0 g, IRON .2 mg, SODIUM 14 mg, and CALC 10 mg

Indian-Style Mangoes

Almost nothing is simpler than this sweet, hot dessert designed for tropical climates.

MAKES 2 SERVINGS

Preparation time: 10 minutes

Chilling time: 15 minutes

1 large ripe mango
½ lime
½ teaspoon curry powder

Slice the mango in half lengthwise around the equater. Twist between your hands to release the pit, which you'll discard. Score the flesh of each half, making a fine crisscross pattern without cutting through the skin. Turn each mango half inside out, and serve on a dessert plate sprinkled with lime juice and curry powder.

Nutritional Analysis: 40 calories, FAT .2 g, PROTEIN .4 g, CARB 11 g, FIBER 1 g,
CHOL 0 g, IRON .2 mg, SODIUM 2 mg, CALC 12 mg

Italian Cheesecake with Raspberries

Leave the crusts to the birds. This tastes great without it.

MAKES 8 SERVINGS

Preparation time: 15 minutes

Cooking time: 1 hour

2 cups part-skim ricotta cheese

3 large eggs

2 tablespoons cornstarch

2 packets aspartame sweetener

1½ teaspoons lemon extract

1 cup fresh raspberries

¼ cup all-fruit red currant preserves

Preheat the oven to 325°F. Butter a 9-inch pie plate. In a large bowl, beat the ricotta and eggs together until smooth. Beat in the cornstarch, sweetener, and lemon extract. Turn into the prepared pie plate. Bake on the middle shelf of the oven for 1 hour, or until a knife inserted in the center comes out clean.

Cool on a wire rack, then chill. Top with fresh raspberries. Melt preserves in a microwave on high (100 percent power) for 30 seconds, then drizzle over the berries. Refrigerate until serving time.

Nutritional Analysis: 145 calories, FAT 7 g, PROTEIN 10 g, CARB 10 g, FIBER 1 g, CHOL 99 mg, IRON 1 mg, SODIUM 102 mg, CALC 195 mg

Lemon Fluff

Here's one of those desserts that slides right down your lovely throat. Easy to make and easy to eat.

MAKES 6 SERVINGS

Preparation time: 10 minutes

Cooking time: 10 minutes

Chilling time: 30 minutes +

2 large eggs, separated

2 cups milk

1 envelope unflavored gelatin

1 packet aspartame sweetener

1 tablespoon sugar

2 teaspoons lemon extract

1 teaspoon grated lemon zest

In a medium saucepan, beat the egg yolks until thick and lemony. Stir in the milk and gelatin and set aside for 5 minutes to soften. Add the sweetener and sugar and cook over low heat, stirring constantly, for 5 minutes. Remove from the heat and stir in the lemon extract and zest. Pour into a large, shallow bowl and chill in a large bowl filled with ice water.

Meanwhile, in a medium bowl, beat the egg whites until soft peaks form. Fold into the lemon mixture. Spoon into six dessert dishes and chill until set.

Nutritional Analysis: 91 calories, FAT 4 g, PROTEIN 5 g, CARB 6 g, FIBER 0.4 g, CHOL 82 mg, IRON .3 mg, SODIUM 65 mg, CALC 105 mg

Vanilla *Pots de Crème*

Simple to make and simply lovely.

MAKES 2 SERVINGS

Preparation time: 10 minutes

Cooking time: 30 minutes

Cooling time: 15 minutes

TO BUTTER AND SUGAR THE RAMEKINS

1 tablespoon butter

½ teaspoon sugar

1 cup heavy cream

1 tablespoon sugar

1 packet aspartame sweetener

Pinch of salt

1 teaspoon vanilla extract

2 large egg yolks

Place a roasting pan filled with 1 inch of water on the middle shelf of the oven. Preheat the oven to 350°F. Butter and sugar two ramekins or glass baking cups.

In a medium bowl, mix together the cream, sugar, aspartame, salt, vanilla, and egg yolks. Stir well, then heat in the microwave on high (100 percent power) for 1 minute. After 1 minute, stir well and return to the microwave for 30 seconds on high (100 percent power). Divide between the two ramekins. Cover the ramekins with foil and place in the roasting pan with warm water. Bake 30 minutes, or until a knife inserted in the middle comes out clean. Cool before serving.

Nutritional Analysis: 277 calories, FAT 27 g, PROTEIN 3 g, CARB 6 g, FIBER 0 g,
CHOL 195 mg, IRON .3 g, SODIUM 51 g, CALC 51 mg

Chocolate *Pots de Crème*

For those nights when you must have chocolate, this will do the trick with minimal guilt.

MAKES 2 SERVINGS

Preparation time: 10 minutes
Baking time: 30 minutes
Cooling time: 15 minutes

TO BUTTER AND SUGAR THE RAMEKINS
1 tablespoon butter
½ teaspoon sugar

1 cup heavy cream
2 teaspoons brown sugar

2 packets aspartame sweetener
2 ounces unsweetened chocolate, broken into bits
1 teaspoon vanilla extract
Small pinch of salt
2 large egg yolks

Place a roasting pan filled with 1 inch of water on the middle shelf of the oven. Preheat the oven to 350°F. Butter and sugar two ¾- or 1-cup ramekins or glass baking cups.

In a medium bowl, mix together the cream, brown sugar, sweetener, chocolate, vanilla, salt, and egg yolks. Stir well. Heat in the microwave on high (100 percent power) for 1 minute. Stir well again and return to the microwave for 30 seconds more on high (100 percent power). Divide between the two ramekins. Cover the ramekins with foil and place in the roasting pan with warm water. Bake 30 minutes, or until a knife inserted in the middle comes out clean. Cool before serving.

Nutritional Analysis: 347 calories, FAT 35 g, PROTEIN 4 g, CARB 9 g, FIBER 2 g, CHOL 195 mg, IRON 1 g, SODIUM 54 g, CALC 64 mg

Gingerbread *Pots de Crème*

For a spicy ending, try the pots de cream with a touch of crystallized ginger.

MAKES 2 SERVINGS

Preparation time: 10 minutes

Baking time: 30 minutes

Cooling time: 15 minutes

TO BUTTER AND SUGAR THE RAMEKINS

1 tablespoon butter

½ teaspoon sugar

1 cup heavy cream

1 tablespoon brown sugar

1 packet aspartame sweetener

1 tablespoon minced crystallized ginger

¼ teaspoon ground cinnamon

⅛ teaspoon ground cloves

⅛ teaspoon ground nutmeg

Small pinch of salt and ground black pepper

2 large egg yolks

Place a roasting pan filled with 1 inch of water on the middle shelf of the oven. Preheat the oven to 350°F. Butter and sugar two ¾- or 1-cup ramekins or glass baking cups.

In a medium bowl, mix together the cream, brown sugar, sweetener, crystallized ginger, cin-namon, cloves, nutmeg, salt, black pepper, and egg yolks. Stir well. Heat in the microwave on high (100 percent power) for 1 minute. Stir well again and return to the microwave for 30 sec-onds more on high (100 percent power). Divide between the two ramekins. Cover the ramekins with foil and place in the roasting pan. Bake for 30 minutes, or until a knife inserted in the middle comes out clean. Cool before serving.

Nutritional Analysis: 277 calories, FAT 27 g, PROTEIN 3 g, CARB 6 g, FIBER .1 g,
CHOL 195 mg, IRON .5 g, SODIUM 60 g, CALC 57 mg

Sugar-Free Almond and Coconut Meringues

Be certain there is not even a speck of grease in your mixing bowl, or the whites won't whip up properly. Store the finished meringues in an airtight tin for 3 or 4 days.

Preparation time: 20 minutes
Baking time: 30 minutes
Resting time: 1 hour in the oven

3 large egg whites
¼ teaspoon kosher salt
3 packets aspartame sweetener
1 teaspoon almond extract
⅓ cup finely chopped almonds
½ cup shredded unsweetened coconut

Preheat the oven to 250°F. In a squeaky-clean bowl, combine the egg whites, salt, and sweetener. Beat with an electric mixer or whisk until the egg whites form stiff peaks. Fold in the almond extract, almonds, and coconut.

Drop by the heaping tablespoon onto a parchment paper–lined baking sheet. Bake 30 minutes, then turn off the oven and allow the meringues to cool in the oven, without opening the door, at least 1 hour. Store in a tin.

Nutritional Analysis: 85 calories, FAT 7 g, PROTEIN 3 g, CARB 3 g, FIBER 2 g,
CHOL 0 mg, IRON .2 g, SODIUM 127 g, CALC 17 mg

RESOURCES FOR HIGH-PROTEIN COOKS

Here are some wonderful prepared foods and basic ingredients that are readily available on the Internet or by phone or mail order.

ARTISAN CHEESES

You might as well eat the best cheeses you can get. There's nothing better for snacks, and to have a sliver of great cheese melting on your tongue makes it all worthwhile. Here are some of our favorites sources:

Sugarbush Farm
591 Sugarbush Farm Rd., Woodstock, VT 05091; 800-281-1757; *www.sugarbushfarm.com.*
Here's the best source for smooth, sharp, artisan Cheddar we love and believe you will, too. Comes in several flavors, our favorite being smoked.

Mozzarella Co.
2944 Elm St., Dallas, TX 75226; 800-798-2954.
For terrific fresh mozzarella as well as a dazzling list of cow, goat, and sheep's milk cheeses, call Paula Lambert.

Vella Cheese Co.
315 Second St., East, Sonoma, CA 95476; 800-848-0505; www.*vellacheese.com.*
Here's a dry grating jack that's nutty sweet, medium-cured, and Parmesan-like. Terrific grated onto all those vegetables you'll eat.

Maytag Dairy Farms
P.O. Box 806, Newton, IA 50208; 800-247-2458.
The source for one of America's great blue cheeses. Great crumbled over a plain grilled steak. No, it wasn't made in a washing machine but, yes, it's the same family.

Dean & Deluca
560 Broadway at Prince, New York, NY 10012; 212-226-6800; *www.deananddeluca.com.*
The premier gourmet grocer of New York not only has an embarrassment of riches in its cheese cases—we adore Spanish manchego, aged Goudas, and others—they also have every single oil or vinegar you could ever imagine.

NATURAL MEATS, SAUSAGES, AND OTHER PURE PROTEINS

Good-quality meat really makes a difference. Here are some of our favorite purveyors. It is worth the trouble to order by phone, mail, or over the Internet if you don't have a good source.

Bruce Aidell's Sausages
Contact Williams-Sonoma, P.O. Box 7456, San Francisco, CA 94120-7456; 800-541-2233.
Or visit a nearby Costco for some of the best low-fat sausages you ever ate. We keep a stock of these sweet, smoky, aromatic sausages in the freezer at all times. Instant joy.

S. Wallace Edwards & Sons

P.O. Box 25, Surry, VA 23883; 800-222-4267;
www.virginiatraditions.com.
Rosy, sweet and salty, dry-cured Virginia hams you can get sliced paper-thin, these brick-red, lean-as-a-Vogue model hams will make you smile.

Sea Bear

P.O. Box 591, Anacortes, WA 98221;
800-645-3474; *www.seabear.com.*
A Northwest hot-smoking technique creates aromatic, sweet, moist, and smoky salmon, oysters, or mussels that come vacuum-sealed in a foil pouch. Throw this in your suitcase if you are going to be stranded for a weekend in some dreadful, fast-food hell.

Dick and Casey's

P.O. Box 2392, Harbor, OR 97415;
800-662-9494; *www.gourmetseafood.com.*
If you're going to eat tuna until you're practically growing gills, treat yourself to the best custom-canned tuna and salmon. This second generation custom packer offers the fish at three salt levels and with four spices. You will want to eat it straight out of the can, it's that good.

Jamison Farm

171 Jamison Lane, Latrobe, PA 15650;
800-237-5262; fax 724-837-2287; *www.jamison-farm.com.*
John and Sukey Jamison hightailed it out of New York to raise their children among lambs in western Pennsylvania. Long known to four-star restaurant chefs as the most reliable source for top-quality lamb, Jamison has everything from chops to butterflied legs. This lamb is the best. We adore it.

ETHNIC INGREDIENTS, HERBS, SPICES, VINEGARS, AND OILS

These distinctive seasonings and flavorings are true labor-savers and most will keep in the pantry or refrigerator for months.

Cinnabar Specialty Foods

1134 W. Haining St., Prescott, AZ 86301;
800-824-4563; *www.cinnabarfoods.com.*
Here's your source for terrific jerk dry rubs and pastes, Thai marinades, tandoori Indian grilling pastes, and more. These products will punch up the flavors of most grilled meats and tofu, too. Known to provide products low in salt, sugars, and fats, this firm's products sizzle with flavor and will expand your horizons.

Wicker's Barbecue Sauce

P.O. Box 126, Hornersville, MO 63855;
800-847-0032.
Here's the barbecue sauce Weight Watcher's classifies as "free." Vinegar-based, it looks like Mississippi River water, but it will flavor a chicken like nothing you ever tried before. Besides the original flavor, you can order mesquite-flavored sauce and a low-sodium version as well as their new Black Label Steak Sauce.

Prairie Herb Farm

P.O. Box 3375, Gillette, WY 82717;
800-447-2867.
Pure, unfiltered herb vinegars that are fat-free, sugar-free, salt-free, and preservative-free—just pure herbs packed into wine vinegars. The flavors are intense. Choose from oregano and garlic, ruby red opal basil and garlic, pineapple sage, chile and peppercorns.

Rising Sun Farms

5126 South Pacific Hwy., Phoenix, OR 97535; 800-888-0795; *www.risingsunfarms.com.* *Fabulous organic products, including specialty oils and vinegars, mustards, and vinaigrettes. Ask for Yum Sauce, fabulous on top of a grilled chop, made from almond butter and other yummy ingredients. Their cheese tortas have won prizes for several years and are heavenly spread onto a celery stick. Their olive oil (organic from California) is the best we know of.*

El Paso Chile Co.

909 Texas Ave., El Paso, TX 79901; 800-274-7468; *www.elpasochile.com.* *Park Kerr's barbecue meat marinade will turn brisket into fine Texas barbecue. And for snacks, try Coyote Nuts, local peanuts roasted and tossed with red chile and garlic. Caramba, that's good. Do try their dry chili mix. It's the real thing. Hold the beans, the way Texans like it.*

Mo Hotta-Mo Betta

P.O. Box 4136, San Luis Obispo, CA 95403; 800-462-3220; *www.mohotta.com.* *Here's the world headquarters for hot. You'll find hot sauces, Jamaican jerk, habanero hot sauces, and gifts of fire. Beware. If you start with these folks, you'll become addicted. They have everything you ever dreamed of—and some things you didn't know to dream for—to sprinkle on meats and vegetables.*

Penzeys Spices

800-741-7787; fax 262-679-7878; *www.penzeys.com.* *Spices sought out from around the world have made Penzey's the largest cataloger of spices and seasonings in the U.S. They offer only highest quality spices from the top growing regions in the world. They grind and blend them in Wisconsin, then pack them in great jars or resealable bags. You'll find more than 250 spices, herbs, and blends here.*

Katagiri

224 E. 59th St., New York, NY 10022; 212-755-3566; fax 212-752-4197; *www.katagiri.com.* *Here's the Japanese grocer to the world. Not only can you order any Japanese ingredient, but you can also pick up Japanese-style kitchen utensils, even incense.*

Zabars

2245 Broadway, New York, NY; 800-697-6301; *www.zabars.com.* *The West Side grocer to New Yorkers, who flock there in droves for everything from smoked fish to Zabar's gear. You want exotic cheese? Oils and vinegars? Tea? Call Zabars. Some say it's the epicurean center of the world.*

INDEX

CONVERSION CHART

Equivalent Imperial and Metric Measurements

American cooks use standard containers, the 8-ounce cup and a tablespoon that takes exactly 16 level fillings to fill that cup level. Measuring by cup makes it very difficult to give weight equivalents, as a cup of densely packed butter will weigh considerably more than a cup of flour. The easiest way therefore to deal with cup measurements in recipes is to take the amount by volume rather than by weight. Thus the equation reads:

1 cup = 240 ml = 8 fl. oz. ½ cup = 120 ml = 4 fl. oz.

It is possible to buy a set of American cup measures in major stores around the world.

In the States, butter is often measured in sticks. One stick is the equivalent of 8 tablespoons. One tablespoon of butter is therefore the equivalent to ½ ounce or 15 grams.

LIQUID MEASURES

Fluid Ounces	U.S.	Imperial	Milliliters
	1 teaspoon	1 teaspoon	5
¼	2 teaspoons	1 dessertspoon	10
½	1 tablespoon	1 tablespoon	14
1	2 tablespoons	2 tablespoons	28
2	¼ cup	4 tablespoons	56
4	½ cup		110
5		¼ pint or 1 gill	140
6	¾ cup		170
8	1 cup		225
9			250, ¼ liter
10	1¼ cups	½ pint	280
12	1½ cups		340
15		¾ pint	420
16	2 cups		450
18	2¼ cups		500, ½ liter
20	2½ cups	1 pint	560
24	3 cups		675
25		1¼ pints	700
27	3½ cups		750
30	3¾ cups	1½ pints	840
32	4 cups or 1 quart		900
35		1¾ pints	980
36	4½ cups		1000, 1 liter
40	5 cups	2 pints or 1 quart	1120

SOLID MEASURES

U.S. and Imperial Measures		Metric Measures	
Ounces	Pounds	Grams	Kilos
1		28	
2		56	
3½		100	
4	¼	112	
5		140	
6		168	
8	½	225	
9		250	¼
12	¾	340	
16	1	450	
18		500	½
20	1¼	560	
24	1½	675	
27		750	¾
28	1¾	780	
32	2	900	
36	2¼	1000	1
40	2½	1100	
48	3	1350	
54		1500	1½

OVEN TEMPERATURE EQUIVALENTS

Fahrenheit	Celsius	Gas Mark	Description
225	110	¼	Cool
250	130	½	
275	140	1	Very Slow
300	150	2	
325	170	3	Slow
350	180	4	Moderate
375	190	5	
400	200	6	Moderately Hot
425	220	7	Fairly Hot
450	230	8	Hot
475	240	9	Very Hot
500	250	10	Extremely Hot

Any broiling recipes can be used with the grill of the oven, but beware of high-temperature grills.

EQUIVALENTS FOR INGREDIENTS

all-purpose flour—plain flour
baking sheet—oven tray
buttermilk—ordinary milk
cheesecloth—muslin
coarse salt—kitchen salt
cornstarch—cornflour

eggplant—aubergine
granulated sugar—caster sugar
half and half—12% fat milk
heavy cream—double cream
light cream—single cream
parchment paper—greaseproof paper

plastic wrap—cling film
scallion—spring onion
shortening—white fat
unbleached flour—strong, white flour
zest—rind
zucchini—courgettes or marrow